T0270114

SHARING TOO MUCH

SHARING TOO MUCH

MUSINGS FROM AN UNLIKELY LIFE

Includes the Worldwide Phenomenon
"How I Saved My Marriage"

#1 *New York Times* and *USA Today* Bestselling Author

RICHARD PAUL EVANS

GALLERY BOOKS
NEW YORK   LONDON   TORONTO   SYDNEY   NEW DELHI

Gallery Books

An Imprint of Simon & Schuster, LLC

1230 Avenue of the Americas

New York, NY 10020

First Gallery Books hardcover edition February 2024

GALLERY BOOKS and colophon are registered trademarks of Simon & Schuster, LLC

Simon & Schuster: Celebrating 100 Years of Publishing in 2024

For information about special discounts for bulk purchases, please contact Simon &
Schuster Special Sales at 1-866-506-1949 or business@simonandschuster.com.

The Simon & Schuster Speakers Bureau can bring authors to your live event. For
more information or to book an event, contact the Simon & Schuster Speakers
Bureau at 1-866-248-3049 or visit our website at www.simonspeakers.com.

Interior design by Erika R. Genova

Manufactured in the United States of America

1 3 5 7 9 10 8 6 4 2

Library of Congress Cataloging-in-Publication Data
Names: Evans, Richard Paul, author.
Title: Sharing too much : lessons from an unlikely life / Richard Paul Evans.
Description: New York City : Gallery Books, 2024.
Identifiers: LCCN 2023012569 | ISBN 9781982177461 (hardcover) |
ISBN 9781982177478 (paperback) | ISBN 9781982177485 (ebook)
Subjects: LCSH: Evans, Richard Paul—Anecdotes. | Authors, American—
20th century—Anecdotes. | Christian authors—United States—
Anecdotes. | BISAC: LITERARY COLLECTIONS / Essays | RELIGION /
Christian Living / Personal Memoirs | LCGFT: Essays. | Anecdotes.
Classification: LCC PS3555.V259 A6 2024 | DDC 813/.54 [B]—dc23/eng/20230717
LC record available at https://lccn.loc.gov/2023012569

ISBN 978-1-9821-7746-1
ISBN 978-1-9821-7748-5 (ebook)

BELIEVE

Believe.

Believe in your destiny and the star from which it shines.

Believe you have been sent from God as an arrow pulled from His bow.

It is the single universal trait which the great of this earth have all shared, while the shadows are fraught with ghosts who roam the winds with mournful wails of regret on their lips.

Believe as if your life depended on it.

For indeed it does.

CONTENTS

SHARING TOO MUCH

BEGINNING

One bright August morning my wife, Keri, called me at my office. She wasn't happy.

"Did you write a blog about our marriage?"

From the tone of her voice, I could guess I was in trouble. "Yes. Why are you asking?"

"They were just talking about it on the local news. You need to take it down."

At that very moment I was in the middle of corresponding with a woman at the *Huffington Post* who was asking for permission to translate my offending blog worldwide into a half dozen languages.

"Why would you want me to take it down?"

"I don't like it. You didn't even ask me if you could share it."

"You've heard me share this in public before," I said. "You were in the front row sitting next to the governor's wife when I shared it with more than a thousand people at the Governor's Marriage Conference. You said you liked it."

"This is different."

"Why is this different?"

"You *wrote* it."

"Why is that different?"

"Because it's *written*," she said.

Hmm. "I don't understand why you're upset. Was any of it not true?"

"That's the problem. It's all true."

"I'm sorry," I said. "I had no idea you didn't like it. And I thought it would help others with their marriages."

"I'm sure it will," she said. "But it's our life. Our life is none of the world's business." Then she said something that gave me pause. "You're too honest. You share too much."

I considered her words for a moment, then said, "I think the world needs more honesty. People respond to my writing because it's true. If I can't write honestly, I'd have to stop writing. And I can't do that. It's who I am. I believe it's my calling."

She thought for a moment before her voice softened. "Fair enough." Then she playfully added, "But if you ever make money off this one, I get it."

The offending blog post, "How I Saved My Marriage," went on to have more than a hundred million readers. Marriage counselors across America told me they've made it required reading for their clients. One of Keri's close friends even called to tell her that the article saved her daughter's marriage.

I'm often asked where the ideas for my books come from.

"Life, mostly," I reply. This book is a compilation of my life as an author, husband, and father—my thoughts and musings over the last half century. Collecting these essays helped me realize just how remarkable my journey has been—an unlikely one for a poor kid from a large family from Utah.

There were some difficult times growing up. Even a few horrific ones, as you'll read. I still hold pain but not resentment. I wouldn't be who I am if it wasn't for those experiences.

Some of what I share is spiritual. I'm not apologizing for this; I'm just forewarning you. These are my experiences and my perception of them. Take or dismiss them as you will.

As most of these stories involve others, I have, in a few instances, changed names and details to protect others' privacy. Keri may be right. Maybe I do share too much. But, then again, maybe if we all were a little more vulnerable the world would be a better place in which to live.

LESSONS
FROM
CHILDHOOD

RICKY THE GREAT

The year I turned eight was a particularly hard one for my family. Our downward spiral began when my father lost his job as a manager of a chain of senior care centers—they called them convalescent centers back then—and was unable to find work. I came from a large family, the seventh of eight children, and things quickly turned desperate. My mother fell into severe depression and started to exhibit suicidal tendencies—something that would haunt her for most of her life. On top of that, this was the year my Tourette's syndrome first manifested and, for reasons I couldn't fathom, my body was ticcing uncontrollably.

With no income, we were forced to sell our home in Arcadia, California, and move to Salt Lake City, Utah, into a dilapidated three-bedroom, rat-infested house that had been abandoned after my grandmother's death. Our new home was in a poor neighborhood just a few blocks from the pawn shops and bars of State Street. My first day at school I learned profanity I had never heard before. I was beaten up three times that year and bullied daily.

The bullying started the week we moved in. Our first weekend in Utah our mother dropped the three youngest of us off at the Avalon movie theater for the Saturday dollar matinee. When the movie was over, a group of boys we'd never seen before—along with a crowd of spectators who I assume had been promised a good show—followed us out to the parking lot.

The ringleader, who was a good head taller than me, started calling my brothers and me names and daring us to fight him. This went on for several minutes before I couldn't stand the humiliation any longer. Even though I wasn't the oldest or the biggest, I clenched my fists and stepped out to fight the bully. Before a punch was thrown, my older brother, who wasn't much bigger than me, pushed me aside and went after the boy. My brother beat him up pretty badly. In the end, the bully was on the ground crying while the crowd he'd gathered mocked him.

As the crowd dispersed, my mother pulled up in our wood-paneled station wagon. The three of us got in the car and went home. We never even told her what had happened.

My parents were pretty much oblivious to our suffering as they struggled with their own challenges, especially financial. My sneakers, with holes in the soles and kite string for shoelaces, left my feet cold in the snow, but I felt too guilty to ask for new shoes. Most days we ate gruel for breakfast—a thin watery cereal made by boiling oatmeal—into which we'd add torn pieces of bread. Struggling to pay the bills, my father worked construction until after dark each night, and in such a small house, I was often privy to stressful conversations my parents had over money. In the throes of her depression, my mother would spend days in the confines of her bedroom. We children were pretty much on our own in a town where everyone just seemed mean. Every day the crossing guard for our school, an angry, desiccated man who looked as old as the small section of road he patrolled, would shout at us for some infraction—walking too fast, too slow, outside the crosswalk, whatever he could growl about.

The meanness extended to my classroom. That year I had a soul-crushing fourth-grade teacher named Mrs. Covey. I'll never forget when, two weeks before Christmas, Mrs. Covey asked who still believed in Santa Claus. Nearly all of us excitedly raised our hands. Mrs. Covey just smirked. "Don't be stupid," she said. "Your parents lied to you. There is no Santa Claus."

Shattered, I walked home and, entering my mother's dark and shuttered room, asked her if there was a Santa Claus. "Santa Claus is the spirit of giving," she said softly.

"But he has reindeer and a sleigh and brings presents down the chimney, right?"

She sighed, then shook her head. "No. There is no Santa Claus."

My heart sank still further at the realization that Mrs. Covey was right. Faith and kindness were supposed to prevail, not cruelty. After a moment I looked back up at my mother and asked, "Did you lie about Jesus, too?"

A few weeks later, two days after being beaten up by an older boy and having my one treasure, a Mickey Mouse watch, stolen, I was turning in an assignment at school when, on a whim, I wrote next to my name:

Ricky Evans *the Great*

I don't know why I wrote it. Clearly, I had no delusions of grandeur. Everything around me testified to my worthlessness. But something about writing those two words next to my name made me feel good, if only for a few seconds.

The next day when we received our papers, I found that Mrs. Covey had erased my two extraneous words and written three of her own:

Shame on you

Then she stood at the front of the classroom and lectured us on the sin of pride, a scolding meant to humiliate and further shame me—the boy who would be great.

That was more than forty years ago. After fourth grade I never saw Mrs. Covey again. She was ancient back then; I'm sure she's long gone now. But I'd like to see her. I'd like to look her in the eyes and say for that innocent little boy, "You were wrong, woman. That little boy was fighting a battle every day and, in spite of fear and neglect and nasty people like you, he not only survived but went on to reach millions of people with his words of hope. He went on to help thousands of abused boys and girls. Ricky Evans *was* great. And you were just mean."

Sadly, there will always be Mrs. Coveys in this world, erasers in hand, eager to blot the greatness from our lives. Don't let them. I'm not advocating hubris or narcissism, but an honest acknowledgment of the beauty and intrinsic worth of each of our souls is something far too many have let the world erase.

GROUNDWATER

Most of my teenage memories of my mother were of her lying in bed in a darkened bedroom. She suffered from depression, complicated by severe hormonal imbalances. It was an era when Valium was handed out like candy to relieve Middle America's housewives of their "anxiety," and those who suffered from depression were just considered weak and sometimes sinful. It would be years before my mother received the help she needed. In the meantime, there was hell to pay.

It was a warm summer evening. I was walking home from a friend's house when I saw all the cars parked in our driveway and around our house. I broke into a run. I opened our front door to find our foyer filled with people—family and neighbors. As I was trying to figure out what was happening, one of my brothers' girlfriends took me aside.

"Why is everyone here?" I asked.

"Your mother slit her wrists. She's dead."

I looked at her in shock. "My mom's dead?"

She nodded. "I'm sorry."

"Where is she?"

"The ambulance just took her."

Thankfully, my mother wasn't dead. The paramedics had stopped her bleeding and gotten her to the hospital in time for lifesaving transfusions. Not surprisingly, she spent the next week in the psych ward. It was a painful and confusing time for a young man.

I never saw the knife she had used to slit her wrists, but there was still a physical reminder. We had an electric knife sharpener in the house. I couldn't tell you the name of my first-grade teacher, but I could draw a detailed picture of that sharpener. It was an avocado-green can opener and knife sharpener in one. It had a small doughnut-shaped magnet that held the can in place as you clamped down on it. It had a slightly sloped plastic appendage on its back with two small slits to run a knife blade through.

Several times, in the weeks following that incident, my mother would go into the kitchen and start sharpening a knife. The shriek of the blade against the sharpening stone could be heard anywhere in the house. I remember hiding behind the couch and covering my ears while each pass of the knife sent shivers through my body.

One night, after my mother had gone to bed, I stole the appliance. I wrapped it in a bath towel and hid it beneath the downstairs bathroom sink.

I like to think that experience taught me empathy. I like to believe I'm a stronger man for it. But every now and then I feel those memories seep up through my thoughts like groundwater. And I realize that deep within me, there is still a shivering little boy covering his ears and hiding behind the couch.

TOURETTE'S SYNDROME

At the age of forty-one I was diagnosed with Tourette's syndrome. It's not that I hadn't suspected that something was wrong with me. I was certain there was. By then I had had more than a dozen different tics—along with the peculiar impulse to shout profanities in public places or spit in the faces of important people. Still, hearing the diagnosis from the doctor had a powerful impact.

"It sounds like you're saying I have Tourette's," I said.

His brow furrowed. "You mean you didn't know?"

His response shook me.

"I knew something was wrong, but I just thought I was weird."

Then something happened that I didn't expect. I began to cry. Not a few tears but a deep, primal sob that rose from my belly. For several moments I just wept. It was embarrassing, really. *Get ahold of yourself*, I thought. *You're a forty-one-year-old man*. Then I realized I wasn't crying for me or my life—I had a great life—but for that lonely little boy who endured years of teasing and torment. Tourette's syndrome is a particularly difficult disorder for children to experience, as it brings ostracism, ridicule, and pain. I remember on many occasions holding my twitching face, hoping the tics would stop. I constantly wondered why I couldn't be normal like the other kids.

As I sat there crying, the wise doctor said, "Richard, your Tourette's is a gift."

I looked up, angry at his comment. *A gift?* I didn't want to be on this man's Christmas list. "You call this a gift?"

"Do you know why I'm seeing you?" he asked.

I thought it was an odd question. He was, after all, a doctor. "I made an appointment," I said.

"I'm a researcher. I don't take patients. But when a colleague of mine told me that she suspected you had Tourette's, I wanted to see if I could help after what you did for me."

"What have I done for you?" I asked. "We've never met."

"More than you can imagine," he replied. "Many years ago, when my wife and I lost our child, my wife didn't think she would ever heal. Your books helped her through her pain. It was your writing that brought her back to me. In her darkest place, she found you. And she felt hope." Then he said something I found profoundly interesting. "Richard, do you think it's a coincidence that you write the books you do—with empathy and sympathy—*and* you have Tourette's?" He shook his head. "No, you write the way you do, not in spite of your Tourette's but precisely *because* you have Tourette's."

It was a life-changing moment for me, one I've considered many times. Oftentimes we succeed not in spite of our challenges and difficulties but because of them. At that moment I realized that, if I had a choice and I could magically live a life without Tourette's and replace my childhood memories with happy, carefree ones or live the life I do now, with the opportunities and experiences I have, I would choose to have the Tourette's.

It's one of life's great ironies. Sometimes our greatest gifts are presented in the packaging of adversity.

THE GRAND BUFFET

A man was looking for a place to eat when he spotted a sign outside a restaurant that read:

ALL-YOU-CAN-EAT BUFFET.
JUST ONE DOLLAR.

He walked inside where he was greeted by another sign that read:

SEAT YOURSELF

The man spied a small table in a crowded corner of the restaurant and sat down. A waitress soon greeted him. "What can I get for you, sir?"

"I'll have the buffet special."

"The special?" she asked.

He looked around the dining room. "Yes, I'll have what everyone else is having."

"All right," she said, handing him a plate. "Help yourself."

There was a long line at the buffet table, and when he got to the food he was disappointed by what he saw. The selection was meager, the quality mediocre, and most of the bins were empty or appeared to have been well picked over.

No wonder it's only a dollar, he thought. He took what he could stomach, then went back to his table grumbling about the food.

After he finished his meal, he went up to the checkout counter to pay. Only as he pulled out his wallet did he notice that there was another room in the restaurant. It was much nicer and less crowded than where he had dined, with crystal chandeliers and beautiful art on the walls. There were long tables laden with food, including many of his favorite dishes: lobster and crab, great roasts and gravies, plump, colorful vegetables, and large platters of cakes, magnificent pastries, chocolate truffles, and desserts of all kinds. A chef stood at one end of the table slicing great slabs of roast beef.

The man asked the waitress, "How much is the buffet in that room?"

"One dollar," she replied.

"It costs the same?"

She nodded. "Everything here is the same price."

"How come you didn't tell me about that room before I ate?"

She looked at him with a nonplussed expression. "Because you said you wanted what everyone else was having."

That is how most people live their lives. Why do we settle for less? I believe, in part, because of fear. We fear risk because we fear the unknown. So we settle into the comfort of the known world and don't sail our ships toward horizons that might turn out to be edges.

We fear risk because we fear failure. The question is, where did we learn that failure is a bad thing? As my father liked to say, "Ships are safe in harbors. But that's not what ships were made for."

Helen Keller spoke well when she said, "Life is either a daring adventure or nothing. Security does not exist in nature, nor do the children of men as a whole experience it. Avoiding danger is no safer in the long run than exposure."

Ralph Waldo Emerson wrote, "Do not be too timid and squeamish about your actions. All life is an experiment. The more experiments you make the better."

Many other great men and women have weighed in on this topic. Friedrich Nietzsche wrote, "A thinker sees his own actions as experiments and questions—as attempts to find out something. Success and failure are for him answers above all."

Thomas J. Watson, the founder of IBM, said, "Would you like me to give you a formula for success? It's quite simple, really. Double your rate of failure. You are thinking of failure as the enemy of success. But it isn't at all. You can be discouraged by failure or you can learn from it. So go ahead and make mistakes. Make all you can. Because remember, that's where you will find success."

Samuel Smiles said, "It is a mistake to suppose that men succeed through success; they much oftener succeed through failures. Precept, study, advice, and example could never have taught them so well as failure has done."

This is my belief. It's okay to fail. But it's not okay to not try. Ironically, often we embrace failure through avoiding it.

I learned that lesson the hard way. My teacher was a young woman named Heather Jennings. Heather Jennings was the most beautiful girl in the ninth grade at Bonneville Junior High School. I can still remember the first time I saw her. It was the last week of school and we were on a field trip. When she walked onto the bus, I practically had a religious experience. I turned to the guy next to me. "Who is that?"

"Heather Jennings. She just moved here." He added, "She's way out of your league."

He didn't have to remind me. I was a poor kid with acne and Tourette's syndrome. I thought about Heather all summer. I wondered what it would be like to have a girlfriend like that. To hold her hand. To kiss her.

Then summer ended and a new school year began. On my first day of high school, I went to one of my classes and sat down in a row of empty seats. A few minutes later Heather Jennings walked in. She looked around the room. Then, to my surprise, she walked over and sat down next to me.

It took me a while to get up enough nerve to talk to her.

After three days, I learned that Heather was not only beautiful but friendly as well. In a moment of rare optimism, I decided I was going to ask her to the homecoming dance. (That was back in the days when you could do it without a helicopter.) Every day I would struggle to summon the courage to ask her, only to lose it when she walked through the door. Finally, just weeks before the dance, I faced the fact that I was running out of time. I committed myself. "No matter what," I told myself, "Monday I'm asking Heather Jennings to the homecoming dance."

Monday morning as I walked to school, I told someone that I was going to ask her. He replied, "You're too late. She's already been asked."

My heart fell. "Who asked her?"

"Tim Wilson."

Tim was the co-captain of the sophomore football team. All the girls loved Tim Wilson.

I was disappointed, but, honestly, also relieved. *Dodged that bullet*, I thought. That was a crazy idea. Heather Jennings was way out of my league.

For the next three years of high school I never forgot Heather. My mouth would go dry when I'd see her in the hall. I even voted for her when she was elected royalty for the senior prom. But that's as close as I got. My dream slowly vanished. I never went out with Heather Jennings. Never kissed Heather Jennings. Never even held her hand.

School ended. Five years later, I was at our high school reunion when Heather Jennings walked into the room. *Still beautiful*, I thought. She smiled when she saw me and walked over. We talked about high school, the lessons of life and the foibles of youth. Then, as she was about to leave, she said, "Do you know what vexed me most about high school?"

"What?" I asked, expecting her answer would have something to do with calculus or Latin or why Mr. Johnson never figured out how to attach his toupee correctly.

"That you never once asked me out. I had the biggest crush on you."

Someone kill me, I thought. Everything I wanted in my life at that time had just been waiting for me. All I had to do was claim it. I had taken counsel from my fears and earned its wage. I vowed that I would never embrace failure through inaction again. It was a life-changing lesson for me, one that has served me well. So even in that failure I came away a better man.

AN OPEN LETTER TO ANONYMOUS

U sually, my fan mail goes to a PO box, to be sorted by my assistant before it comes to me. It's one of the ways I keep my life as an author separate from my personal life. So I was surprised to find a handwritten envelope addressed to Richard Paul Evans sent directly to my home address. The letter had no name or return address.

As I read the letter, my anger rose. The writer had heard me speak at a church. The letter said I had no right to be in a church, since I was clearly a sinful man, manifested by my facial tics—something I've had since childhood.

At first I crumpled the letter and threw it away. Then, after thinking about it, I decided to answer it. The problem was, the letter was anonymous, so I had no way of reaching the writer. I couldn't even know for sure if the writer was a man or a woman, though I assumed the latter from the feminine handwriting and stationery.

Then I had an idea. I'd post my response on Facebook

and ask my readers if they would share it. That's the power of social media. With enough shares, there was a reasonable chance she might actually see it.

I posted my letter around midnight. The next morning, I checked my computer to see if anyone had noticed my posting. To my astonishment, it already had more than eighty thousand likes and tens of thousands of shares. The letter had clearly hit a nerve. There were hundreds of comments, some more than a page long, with people sharing their sympathy and outrage.

This is what I wrote:

> *Dear Anonymous,*
>
> *I was very much disheartened by your letter. I was saddened that you hadn't the courage to include your name so I could help you understand the truth. Since I must believe that you wouldn't possibly friend a "man like me" on your Facebook page, I can only hope that someone you know shares this post on their page and that God guides you to this letter.*
>
> *I came to your church to tell you about God's love for His children and to talk about the beauty and power of His grace. I don't think you heard me. Or, at least, believed me. You wrote in your letter that I had no place in a house of God, as I was clearly a sinful man and that my sins were manifested across my face, revealed by my facial tics.*
>
> *Yes, there's no doubt that I am, like the rest of God's children, a sinner. But the tics you saw on my face*

were not caused by sin. They come from a neurological disorder called Tourette's syndrome. I was born with them. I cannot stop them.

Sadly, as a boy, I would have believed you. My mother got mad at me that day my first tic manifested—a painful, constant shrugging. And, though I was only eight years old, I felt guilty for disobeying her when she told me to stop. As a nine-year-old I thought that maybe, if I was a good enough boy and I had enough faith, I could be cured of my tics. But they wouldn't go away, so I thought it was my fault.

One time a church leader came to speak at my church. The adults at my church said that he was someone important. I remembered the Bible story of the woman touching Jesus's garment and being healed. I thought that maybe if I shook this man's hand I might be healed. So I waited in line and I shook his hand. But my tics remained.

Earlier that summer, my family had moved to Utah and I had ridden a school bus to an overnight camp called Mill Hollow. Some of the children on the bus noticed my tics and one of them called me a "freak." As I got off the bus—a scared child in a strange place—a group of children surrounded me to get a better look. And I was ticcing like crazy, not because I was a sinner but because I was afraid and humiliated.

Your letter reminded me a little of that day. Only I am no longer that helpless little boy. I now know that there are hundreds of thousands of us with behavioral disorders. And what you, or even a million people like you, might say, doesn't affect me anymore. I have moved on. I have a beautiful life, a beautiful family and home. I have seen the world. I have danced in the White House and spoken to audiences of thousands. Tens of millions of people have read my books and watched my movies. I have built shelters that have housed tens of thousands of abused children. And I still tic.

Sometimes when I tic, my wife will lovingly lay her hand on my cheek and ask if I'm okay. It's very sweet. And it means a lot to me. My children don't even notice my tics. They only see the father who loves them. The truth of who I am has set me free. It can set you free too. Because with whatever measurement you use to judge, you must judge yourself. And you are using a very barbed ruler.

In all honesty, I must admit that I was angered by your letter. But not for me. I am beyond your reach. I am angry for those children who are still trying to figure out who they are: children who are teased and ridiculed and bullied by cruel, self-righteous people like you. I am angered for those sweet, innocent children, who would rather die than show their tics, because you are so eager to let them know how unlovable and imperfect they are. And some of them do take their precious lives. Yes, this makes me very angry.

The other day, at a book signing, a young woman I had never met before put her arms around me and told me that she loved me. I asked her why. She told me *that she had Tourette's syndrome and the kids at school made fun of her. But now many of her schoolmates are reading my books and, knowing that I have Tourette's, are now treating her better. I told her that she is not her Tourette's. I told her that I loved her too.*

Dear Anonymous, I hope you read this letter. I hope it opens your eyes. Or better yet, your heart. But whether you change or not, remember this: we, the "abnormal," are not the ones to be pitied. The greatest disability is the inability to love those who are different from you. May God bless you with His unfathomable and unconditional love.

> *Your flawed servant,*
> *Richard Paul Evans*
> *#1 New York Times bestselling author and*
> *a man with Tourette's syndrome*

I never heard from the woman. But I did hear from thousands of caring, sympathetic people. I was glad I wrote it.

THE FOLLY OF YOUTH

W hen I was twelve, I thought my neighbor's father was the coolest of the cool—a modern Jay Gatsby. "Cool Dad #1," I'll call him, had two cars: a beautiful Mercedes-Benz and a candy-apple-red convertible Jaguar. He had an industrial car wash system installed in his garage, so his cars always looked shiny and new. The home also had an indoor swimming pool. He was the co-owner of a golf resort, wore expensive suits, and would say cool things to his son like, "Hey, it's bedtime, sport. Go directly to bed, do not pass Go, do not collect two hundred dollars."

One time he took his son and me to a professional basketball game. His son was bored and whined that he had to go, but it was a pretty big deal for me, not just to go to my first professional basketball game but to sit in VIP seats.

As we arrived at the arena, Cool Dad #1 told us that he had a special reserved parking space. He parked his Mercedes in a no-parking zone directly in front of the arena's entrance and crumpled up the parking ticket when we came out.

My family's situation was different. A lot different. My father was a social worker, a part-time marriage counselor, and a struggling home builder. Our financial situation was always stressful. Unlike the impeccably dressed Cool Dad #1, my father would come home from work in concrete-stained Levi's and old shirts spattered with dried paint and plaster. The only reason we were able to live in the same neighborhood as Cool Dad #1 was that my father got a deal on a corner lot and our family built the house from the ground up—from pouring the foundation and framing the walls to putting up and taping drywall. My bedroom didn't have paint the first year, and there was no carpet or flooring when we moved in.

Then, as if life weren't hard enough for my parents, my father fell on a construction site and broke both legs. We had neither health insurance nor savings, and now we had no income. We were forced to sell our home and move the ten of us into a three-bedroom duplex. I slept on the floor for nearly two years.

Several years later, our financial situation began to improve, and we built a house in a new neighborhood—one a bit humbler than where we'd previously lived. We had been there for almost a year when Cool Dad #1 was all over the evening news. He had been indicted for mail, securities, and bankruptcy fraud and sentenced to ten years in prison. He had defrauded some 650 investors out of more than $20 million. Many of these investors lost their entire life savings. Ironically,

I suppose, one of those investors was a new neighbor of ours. Shortly after losing his retirement savings, he hanged himself in his garage.

This was not the only failure of my youthful judgment. In high school I dated a popular girl with another "cool" father. Cool Dad #2 was fast-talking and arrogant and knew how to wow my simple young mind. Occasionally he'd take us to dinner at nice restaurants—something our family couldn't afford (except when we went to the restaurant where my mother washed dishes). Cool Dad #2 drove a nice car, wore custom cowboy boots, and sported a handful of gaudy gold rings. He even had a billboard with his name on it, which I thought made him famous. It wasn't until I was an adult that I learned that, behind closed doors, Cool Dad #2 was a monster. He was both physically and mentally abusive, and was not only a wife and child beater but a serial cheater as well.

Unlike the two Cool Dads, my father was quiet, hardworking, and honest. He was not good with money, nor did he ever make much of it. For years he drove an old van he bought used from the telephone company's public auction. He had no close friends and no hobbies other than to provide for his large family.

On the outside, the contrast between my father and these two men was clear to everyone. But what really mattered was not what the world could see; it was character. I thank God that my father was unlike both of those men I once foolishly admired. The Cool Dads were bad men.

The problem with youth is that without life experience they are blinded by bling, enamored of the world's highlight films while witnessing—in the privacy of their homes—the blooper reels. The truth is naturally less appealing than the show.

The rabbi, theologian, and philosopher Abraham Joshua Heschel said, "When I was young, I admired clever people. Now that I am old, I admire kind people." Amen. And amen.

THE CAGE

My mother always wanted to be a writer. I suppose that's why she read so many books to me. For as long as I can remember, she talked about an Erma Bombeck–style book she planned to write called *Rocks in My Head: A Memoir on Motherhood.* But some of her older siblings told her she wasn't good enough and sadly she believed them. She wasn't strong that way.

My mother was born into a poor Mormon family of thirteen children: eleven girls, two boys. She was the last of the brood, and you would think her parents would have run out of names by then, but in fact, they gave her three: June Sue Carol.

I never really knew my maternal grandparents. I've only seen old black-and-white photos of them. My grandfather died shortly after I was born, and I have only one memory of my grandmother; even that seems to be in black and white.

My mother and her sisters were nearly as fruitful as their mother. I have more than a hundred first cousins on my mother's side. People I don't know come to my book signings and tell me they're my cousins and I believe them.

When I was a teenager, I asked my mother why she had so many children. She replied, "I don't know. We never really thought about it. It's just what you did."

Even back then her answer bothered me. Maybe it's because too many of us live our lives trapped in cages of cultural paradigm and make the big life decisions by default. It's just the way it is. Our cultural cage feels safe. Miserable and cramped, but safe.

After my mother's death I found boxes filled with writings she had never shown anyone. She had a beautiful literary voice. She could tell stories. She could have been a writer.

But not everyone lives that way. Some people escape the paradigm cage. It takes courage to fly away. It takes faith that there might be something better out there. Spoiler alert: there is.

TO GERDY AND BEAU, WITH LOVE

(A TRIBUTE TO THE DOGS IN MY LIFE)

My wife just got a dog. His name is Beau. He's a little cavapoo—one of those fancy poodle mixes. He has soft, kinky, hypoallergenic fur with markings like a Holstein cow, black and white with brown eyebrows and a big black spot over one of his eyes. He's adorable.

Keri said she wanted a dog to keep her company when I'm gone. (This sounds like I'm dying. As far as I know, I'm not.) The truth is, I'm not gone as much as I used to be, back in the early days of my career when authors still did book tours. I think she feels this way because the kids are all gone so now, when I'm away, it's unusually quiet around the house.

What is most surprising to me about Keri's decision is that she was never a dog person. When we were dating, she told me she never wanted a dog in our house, which was nearly a deal breaker for me. She grew up with a dog, a yappy little Yorkshire terrier named Fred. They say that dogs take on their owners' personalities and, in this case, it was true. Fred was Keri's father's dog. Her father was a gruff little Italian man, a union negotiator for a copper mine. The first time I went home with Keri both her father and his dog growled at me.

Beau wasn't actually the dog Keri was planning to get. She had found a cavapoo breeder online who gave the litter temporary names based on Disney characters. The dog she'd picked out had been named Buzz, after Buzz Lightyear. When we got to the breeder to meet her dog, Buzz was, in Keri's words, a buzzkill. He barely responded to her attention.

There were a half dozen dogs in the litter and one of the others, named Tarzan, was a different story. Maybe it's true that dogs pick their owners, but Tarzan, aka Beau, pranced over and wouldn't stop licking me. I handed him to Keri and he kept licking her face. The choice was obvious. After much consideration, she named him Beau, as in Beau Brummel. (That's okay, I didn't know who that was either.) We brought him home for Christmas.

When I was nine, my brother and his girlfriend gave me a dog for my birthday. I have no idea what breed it was—a mix of some kind—but she was small and cute with short golden hair. They had named her Gerdy Grouch. It was an awful name, but I was only nine and it hadn't occurred to me that I could change it, so Gerdy she remained. The timing of the gift was perfect. We had just moved into a run-down neighborhood in a rat-infested home in Utah. It was a horrible time of life.

My family was in crisis, and I had no friends and an abusive schoolteacher. I was bullied and beaten up on a regular basis.

But I had Gerdy to come home to. Together we would explore the undeveloped acres of fields around us. She was always at my side. We had two other dogs: my sister's, a Pomeranian named Honey, and my brother's, a mutt named Chester.

Things began to look up for our family and we moved out of that rotten neighborhood. A year later, one day before school, my mother asked me to get the dogs in. I went outside and called for Gerdy, who was across the street playing with Chester. As always, Gerdy came as soon as I called. I didn't see the car coming down the street, but she ran right in front of it. I could see her little body falling under the car as it passed, leaving her lying in the road. The car stopped as I ran to her. Gerdy was still alive, but on her side writhing in pain. I picked her up and cradled her in my arms. She licked me on the mouth, then died. I remember sitting in the road holding my little friend when the lady walked up to me.

"Is that your dog?"

It was an inane question. I couldn't answer. I just looked up with my arms full, my chin quivering, and tear-filled eyes.

"I'm sorry," she sputtered, "but it ran in front of me. I couldn't stop in time." She stood there awkwardly for a moment, then got back in her car and drove away.

With tears streaming down my cheeks, I carried my little dog home. To this day I don't understand my mother's response, but she reacted poorly. Coldly. "You need to go to school," she said. "You can bury her when you get home."

I laid Gerdy by the side of the house, covered her with her

blanket, then washed my face and walked to school. At lunch-time I didn't eat. I went outside on the school lawn, as far away from anyone as I could, and cried until the bell rang.

For months I mourned Gerdy. It was my first taste of death of someone close to me, and the bitterness seemed more than I could bear. Gerdy was the only dog I'd ever owned. I don't know why. Maybe I didn't want to feel that loss again. We had other dogs, family dogs, but none that were just mine.

A reporter once asked me why I wrote stories that made people cry. I had to think about it. Then I replied, "The stories that stayed with me as a child were the ones that made me cry. Stories like *Old Yeller* and *Where the Red Fern Grows*." I suppose it's no coincidence that both of those stories were about dogs.

Beau has bonded to Keri. He jauntily follows her around the house like a shadow. When she goes to bed, he finds a nook in her position and curls up into her. I don't know why, but it brings me unspeakable joy. Since I go to bed later than Keri, I come in, scoop Beau up (after scratching his belly, which he always wants), and put him in his crate. I then let him out in the morning, at which time he immediately jumps on the bed and licks Keri's face. Almost every day, Keri wakes laughing. It's a joyful way to start the day. Beau has brought remarkable happiness into our home.

Dogs are wonderful that way. They are wonderful teachers. They are practically synonymous with loyalty. And love. I wish I could love like Beau does. Like Gerdy did. *Canis familiaris* has the remarkable ability to love unconditionally, something we could all use a lot more of in our lives. I think the world needs more dogs.

TO MY MOTHER

On the morning of Valentine's Day 2006 I lost my biggest fan. My mother, June Sue Carol Thorup Evans, died quietly in her home. One of my first memories is of me, at the age of three, climbing a tetherball pole and from the top of the pole calling to her, "Look, Mom. Look! I made it to the top!" I did the same thing after my first book hit number one on the bestseller list. "Look, Mom. Look! I made it to the top!" I always wanted her to be proud of me.

The first book I wrote, an international bestseller called *The Christmas Box*—a story about a mother's love and the loss of a child—helped heal my mother of the pain she held from the loss of her daughter Sue. My mother was pleased I had written it. In fact, she helped me share it.

When I first self-published my little book, my mother was working as a receptionist for a physical therapist. Few patients left the clinic without a copy of my book. She made sure of that. Every few days she'd call me for more copies to sell. She helped me take my first steps as a child and she helped me take my first steps as an author.

More difficult for her to share were the stories of the dark times when she suffered from depression. For a while she became suicidal and more than once attempted to take her life. I promised my mother I would not print anything about her without her permission. She struggled with the thought of sharing such personal challenges with the public but, even more, with her own family. In the end she said, courageously, "We should share my story. It might help someone in their own struggles."

It did. Thousands of women no longer felt so alone in their pain. They sent her flowers and, at book signings, asked me to thank her.

When I was a child, my mother insisted that I learn how to speak well in public. I remember, at the age of nine, a Saturday afternoon sitting at the kitchen table memorizing a full-page talk to give in church the next day. It was a beautiful fall day and I desperately wanted to be outside hunting grasshoppers with my new BB gun. I also knew that most people just read their talks at church. But my mother wanted me to learn to speak in public and insisted that I do my best.

Since then I have spoken to tens of thousands of people worldwide, from Melbourne, Australia, to Lisbon, Portugal, and shared the podium with presidents, prime ministers, and movie stars. How grateful I am for my mother's insistence that I learn to speak in public.

Most of all, my mother was a hero. She nearly died giving

birth to her first child and was warned by her doctor that she would not be so fortunate the second time. But she believed there were more children to come and risked her life seven more times. I was the seventh child.

After her passing, I was the first of the children to arrive at her side. I knelt by her bed and wept. After a few minutes I noticed an unopened Valentine's Day card from my father next to her bed. I opened it. It read, "To the woman who believed in me more than I believed in myself."

I miss my mother. A year after her death I got some good news from my publisher and asked my assistant to get my mother on the phone. My assistant paused a moment, then said, "Rick, you know I can't do that."

Confused by her response, I replied, "Of course you can; just call her."

She looked at me sadly, then said, "No, Rick. I can't."

Then I remembered. My assistant touched my hand kindly. "I'm sorry. We always want to tell our moms when something important happens."

Yes, we do.

FAITH, CHRISTMAS, AND MIRACLES

PREMONITIONS

Early in my writing career, when I was my own publisher, I was in San Diego, driving myself from a book signing, navigating a rental car on unfamiliar roads looking for my hotel. I was lonely, hungry, and tired. I was also discouraged, as the book signings had been a bust. I had signed only one book and that was to the bookstore's owner.

Suddenly I had a distinct premonition that I needed to pull into a parking lot ahead of me. Without knowing why, I followed the prompting. I had no sooner parked when there was a knock at my window. I turned to see a woman standing outside. She was dressed in tattered clothing. Two small children were huddled close to her. I cracked open my door. "May I help you?"

"Excuse me, sir," she said, "my children are hungry. I was wondering if you could feed them tonight."

The children hid their faces from me in their mother's coat.

"Of course," I said.

That evening I bought dinner for Mary, Angel, and Bobby at a Jack in the Box drive-through, then drove off to find my hotel.

Another time I was in Salt Lake City when I felt the premonition to visit Stacy (not her real name), a young divorced woman who went to my church. Eager to accomplish all I had to do that morning, I tried to push the thought aside. But the premonition remained. *Visit Stacy*, the prompting came.

Finally, I turned my car around and drove to Stacy's house. I walked up and rang the doorbell. Nothing. I knocked. Still nothing.

Thinking I must have just had a false premonition, I started to walk away. As I got to my car I heard a sound. I looked back. The door was partially ajar. I walked back.

"Stacy?"

I put my ear to the door and heard a slight whimper. "Stacy?" I opened the door. Stacy was lying on the tile floor of the foyer. She had been raped by her ex-husband.

Over the next few months, I escorted her to the court proceedings as she faced her assaulter. One time she collapsed from fear on the way to court and I literally ended up carrying her into the courthouse. I was glad I could be there for her.

Whatever the source of these voices or promptings, they feel external. I've felt the power of them. I think most of us have had feelings like these from time to time. The ultimate question, I suppose, is what we do with them.

NOT MY DAY TO DIE

The trip that I had planned to the Caribbean seemed cursed from the onset. I wanted to surprise my wife, Keri, with something she'd never done before, and a friend recommended a Caribbean cruise. So that December I gave Keri the twelve days of Christmas, each day presenting her with a gift and a new tile from Scrabble, spelling out her surprise. T-H-E C-A-R-I-B-B-E-A-N. She didn't figure out where we were going until the second to last day, when she got a tile with a pirate's eye patch.

She was excited to go and we prepared for our trip for months. Then, just six hours before our flight, I received a call from my brother. My father, who had been sick for several months, was dying. The trip was canceled.

The next Christmas I again gave Keri Scrabble letters. This time the tiles spelled out L-E-T-S T-R-Y A-G-A-I-N. Again, Keri was thrilled and three weeks later we flew from SLC to Atlanta, then on to the island of St. Martin, where we boarded the *Wind Spirit*, a small cruise ship with only 128 passengers. We sailed to St. Kitts, Tortola, Virgin Gorda and, on the last day, our favorite of the islands, St. Barts—a French territorial collectivity.

Some friends we'd made on the cruise, Sharon and Randy, had invited us to join them on a beautiful white-sand beach called Flamands, so we spent the day sunning and swimming in the picturesque Windex-blue waters. After lunch, Sharon and I swam out to bodysurf. Keri decided the waves were too big, so she stayed on the beach to read.

It was nearly time to go when I decided to catch one last wave. That's when things went bad. Really bad. As I caught the wave, I was sucked down under the crest and tumbled through the surf like a sock in a dryer.

Then I hit something. My stop was as abrupt as a head-on collision. I heard a loud *snap* and searing pain shot through my body. I knew I was in serious trouble—I just didn't know what kind.

It's amazing to me how quickly our thoughts move during an accident. My first thought was that I had broken my neck and I began imagining what it would be like to be paralyzed. Or was this the end of my life? If I was paralyzed, surely I would drown. My most peculiar thought was, *At least it's a beautiful place to die.*

I had just gotten my head above water when another wave hit me, this time pushing me facedown into the sand. When I got my head above water again, I desperately gasped for air, which was not only excruciatingly painful but nearly impossible. (I learned later that I had difficulty breathing because I had broken all my ribs.) Then the tide began pulling me out to sea.

At that moment I had an experience I'll never forget. A voice clearly said to me, "Fight for your life or you will die today." I dug my knees and elbows into the sand and began dragging myself onto the beach. The experience took on a dreamlike quality. In the distance I heard Sharon say, "I think Richard's hurt . . ." to which Randy replied, "Nah, he's just playing around." I couldn't call for help. I couldn't even speak; I still hadn't taken a full breath. That's when I blacked out.

When I woke, Randy was sitting in the sand next to me. "I'm hurt," I said.

"We know," he said.

"Am I paralyzed?" I blacked out again.

The next thing I remembered was a young French woman kneeling over me, wiping sand off my body. "Who are you?" I asked. She replied in broken English, "Ai-li-hee." I blacked out again.

The next time I woke, Keri was at my side. She asked if I knew what was wrong. I told her I had heard something snap. Then the paramedics arrived. Oddly, they just told me to stand. I couldn't, so they lifted me to my feet and walked me to the ambulance, where I was strapped onto a cot.

The St. Barts "hospital" was little more than a clinic. The nurse spoke a little English, the doctor spoke none. They gave me Tramadol, a narcotic painkiller, then took me to another room for X-rays. The radiologist accidentally slammed my wheelchair into a door frame, which elicited a stifled scream from me.

A few minutes later the doctor came to me with a dictionary that he had opened to the word *scapula*. "Broke," he said. "Broke." He gave me Tylenol for the pain and Keri stopped at a pharmacy in town for a splint for my shoulder. Then we waited at the pier for our ship's tender to arrive. I was helped onto the boat and taken to the ship's doctor, who gave me some morphine.

That night I dreamt over and over of being tumbled in the waves. Keri got up several times to take care of me. The next day we disembarked in St. Martin. I should be clear that I'm not a fan of St. Martin—I'm not exaggerating when I say that everyone Keri and I encountered, from those at the airline counter to the store owners, was not only unhelpful but downright hostile. This was particularly bad since we had to wait at the airport for an excruciating eight hours.

As the morphine wore off, it started to make me itch. I was in severe pain and not sure how I would endure the cramped flight to Atlanta. I said a silent prayer for help, then tried to upgrade to first class, which the woman at the airline counter wouldn't even consider.

Then she added that because I was hurt, I needed to be moved out of the exit row. I asked if there were any rows on the plane that weren't full and she said, "No, the economy section is completely sold out."

To make matters even worse, our flight was delayed, and we were told we would likely miss our connection, meaning we would have to spend the night in Atlanta. It seemed like the universe was conspiring to increase my suffering.

To our relief, our flight arrived sooner than expected, and

Keri and I filed onto the crowded plane with the other passengers. Then, with a seat still open between us, the flight attendants closed the door. Unbelievably, Keri and I had the row to ourselves. After takeoff I lay with my head in Keri's lap and slept nearly the whole flight. It was a tender mercy.

We made our connection in Atlanta and arrived home in Salt Lake City a little past midnight. We drove directly to the ER, where they put me through a more advanced series of X-rays. When the doctor came in he said, "Richard, you do things big, don't you? That's the worst break I've ever seen on anyone living." When I told him we had just flown in from the Caribbean he replied, "If this had happened locally, you would have been in our trauma unit. I can't believe you survived that flight home."

As he showed me my X-rays, I noted an uneven white line crossing my ribs. "What's that?" I asked.

"You broke all your ribs," he said. "You're very lucky you didn't puncture your lungs. You wouldn't be here if you had."

The next day a CT scan showed that the force of impact had driven my humerus through its socket, fracturing the socket and shattering the scapula into dozens of pieces. The doctor was vexed. "I'm afraid that if I open up your shoulder, the bone will just crumble," he said. "As it is, it's being held in place by muscle. I believe that if we keep it splinted it will heal correctly on its own."

As I look back on the experience, I can't help but believe that I was divinely protected that day. Had I hit just slightly differently, my neck would have snapped. In fact, a few months later a friend of my agent drowned in the same sea. My agent said, "It makes me sick every time I think about how close I came to losing you."

I was protected in the waves that day and have a heart full of gratitude for the angels under the water and the human angels on the beach who delivered me home alive. By all rights, I should have died under the waves. I guess it just wasn't my day to die.

WHAT I LEARNED IN PRISON

I once posted on Facebook a letter I received from a man serving life in prison for first-degree murder. He expressed gratitude to me that my books had helped him through his darkest and most hopeless moments. Though I received more than a thousand "likes" and dozens of comments from fans about my post, one woman's comment in particular struck me.

"[That criminal] shouldn't have a book that takes him from the punishment that his actions brought upon him . . . anything that can act like a cheerleader to raise his spirits seems contrary to doing his penance and making payment to society . . . I quite frankly don't give one rats [sic] ass how his day-to-day spirits are . . ."

A few people "liked" her comment. More were repulsed. One man wrote, "Do you have any idea how sick you sound?"

The woman responded, "You're judging me? I didn't realize that Jesus was hiring."

I finally responded to the increasingly hostile thread with part of Matthew 25:36: "I was in prison and you visited me . . ."

Honestly, I can't judge this woman. Perhaps she was a victim of a violent crime or had lost a loved one to murder. Under such circumstances, maybe I would have felt the same.

I receive a lot of mail from prison. I have also spoken in prisons a half dozen times or more. The first time I spoke, I had an experience I never expected—one that I'll never forget.

After passing through the security check, the guards pointed out where I was speaking and I walked to the building alone, falling in with a line of prisoners—me in a dark business suit, they in their cotton jumpsuits.

The room was packed with felons. In fact, just before I began my talk, the pastor who had invited me to speak informed me that the men were "pretty much all murderers." Despite my trepidation, the words came effortlessly. Then, a few minutes into my talk, something very peculiar happened— something that's a little difficult to explain and perhaps even more difficult to believe.

A powerful feeling came over me—one that was so strong that my legs weakened and I had to lean on the lectern to support myself. It wasn't fear or anxiety I was feeling; it was the opposite. It was an intense feeling of love—not from me but from some external force.

The feeling took my breath away. For a moment I stopped speaking and just looked out over the men. Then I asked, "Can you feel that?"

The men just looked at me.

I said, "This is remarkable. I can feel the love that God has for you . . ."

A few of the men wiped their eyes from emotion. After my talk I embraced nearly every one of those men. (I was informed later that physical contact wasn't allowed.) Afterward, I told the pastor what I had felt. He nodded with understanding. "I've felt that before," he said. "It's a remarkable feeling." Then he added, "We don't ever stop loving our children, do we?"

As I walked out of the prison it occurred to me that if God loved these felons so powerfully—these men who had done horrible things—why, then, do we sometimes question God's love because of our own foibles and failed natures? That night I realized that experience had been a gift—a beautiful gift of understanding. Something, perhaps, I could have learned only in prison.

ARE THE DYING VISITED BY THE DEAD?

S itting on the bed next to my grandmother as she lay dying, I witnessed a curious thing. Earlier that day, hospice had put her on a morphine drip, and ever since I'd arrived, she had seemed unaware of her surroundings and was mumbling unintelligibly.

Then she abruptly stopped mumbling and looked up at the corner of the room. For more than a minute she was silent and her eyes were focused on a single point. Then, very clearly, she said, "No, not yet." She died several hours later.

While there is much debate about what happens during the final minutes of life, reported end-of-life "visitation experiences" are extremely common. In my speaking, I've had the opportunity to address hundreds of hospice workers. Never once has any of them told me they don't believe that the dying have visitations. If anyone would know, it would be them. So why isn't this phenomenon addressed more openly?

When my father-in-law, a confessed atheist, was on his deathbed from a terminal heart ailment, his eyes suddenly widened. Because of the tube down his throat he was unable to speak but he was clearly lucid, following something across the room with his eyes. Keri was at his side. "Dad, do you see someone?"

He nodded in the affirmative.

"Is it Grandma?"

He shook his head.

"Do you know who it is?"

Again he shook his head.

Minutes after his passing, his nurse said to me, "I knew he was going to die soon. When they start getting visitations, it's their time." I asked if she'd seen this before. She nodded. "Frequently."

Reported end-of-life experiences are predominantly categorized as three types: out-of-body experiences (OBEs), near-death experiences (NDEs), and end-of-life dreams and visions (ELDVs).

In a study of end-of-life phenomena, scientists at Canisius University interviewed sixty-six patients receiving end-of-life care in a hospice. The study found that most patients reported at least one vision per day— and that visions involving dead friends and relatives were the most common.

The researchers wrote, "As participants approached death, comforting dreams/visions of the deceased became more prevalent. The impact of pre-death experiences on dying individuals and their loved ones can be profoundly meaningful . . . and typically lessen the fear of dying, making transition from life to death easier for those experiencing them."

Still, despite the myriad written accounts of pre-death encounters, there are still many who don't believe. Afterlife deniers have offered a list of possible scientific explanations for end-of-life phenomena that include excess carbon dioxide creating a white light and tunnel, endorphins released under stress, lack of oxygen, hallucinations and a damaged temporoparietal junction, which may create the illusion of an out-of-body experience—a phenomenon that scientists claim to have been able to replicate without bringing the body close to death.

However, none of these explain how people brought back from death are able to explain things that happened in other rooms, such as conversations and unseen visitors. A prime example of this is the well-documented case of "Maria." After being resuscitated from a heart attack, Maria told a social worker that during the time her heart had stopped she had left her body and gone outside the hospital. She described in detail an orange sneaker she'd seen on the ledge of a window on the third floor. The doubtful but curious social worker decided to explore Maria's claim. Not only did she find the sneaker but she also realized that there was no other way for Maria to have seen the sneaker or its surroundings that she had described.

Many scientists believe that as medical advances allow us to bring more people back from death, we will see and validate more of these experiences. I believe that for those seeking truth about the existence of an afterlife, an honest inquiry into end-of-life phenomena is a good place to start.

VISIONS

H ave you ever had a "vision"? In evoking the word, I don't mean a future goal or motivational hope but rather an actual supernatural experience. We live in a world that's skeptical about spiritual gifts, yet I can't deny my own experiences. I would be lying if I did.

My first vision came to me when I was in my mid-twenties. At the time, I owned a struggling animation company called ClayMagic Productions. We'd procured our first large client, Dentsu Inc., an advertising and PR agency out of Tokyo, who had asked us to create a commercial for one of the largest food companies in Japan. We had spent weeks building a set for the commercial, but I didn't know how to create the animation the client had requested—a group of angel pies (a popular Japanese treat resembling a MoonPie) holding hands and dancing, then jumping into the air. I had no idea how to make this happen in stop-frame animation without visible supports.

One afternoon, as our deadline for shooting the scene loomed, my production manager walked into my office. "We need to start shooting the dancing scene tomorrow morning," he said. "Did you figure out how to do the animation?"

I shook my head. "Not yet."

"We don't have much time left," he said anxiously, then left.

Not knowing what to do, I began to pray. That's when I had a vision. I saw, very clearly, an oddly shaped frame to hold the figures while we animated them. I quickly sketched what I saw in my vision, then walked out and gave the plans to my production manager. "Try this."

He looked over my drawing and said, "Where did you get this?"

"It just came to me," I said. "Let's try it."

Following the plans I'd sketched, my production manager built the device. After he set up the camera to shoot the scene, he came back to my office. "That thing you designed is genius," he said. "Every time one of the supports is about to come into view, one of the characters moves in front of it to conceal it. You're brilliant."

It wasn't me. I didn't even know if it would work.

My second vision was even more remarkable. The first book I wrote was called *The Christmas Box*, which remarkably went on to become a number one international bestseller. At the heart of the story is a woman grieving her deceased child at the base of an angel statue.

The angel statue I wrote about actually exists in the downtown Salt Lake City Cemetery. People come from all over the world to see it, leaving notes, flowers, and toys at the statue's base. On one occasion I was visiting the statue when I found on the monument's granite base a homemade Easter card that read:

> *My sweet little girl,*
> *I hope there are Easter dresses where you are.*
>
> *Love, Mommy*

I was moved by the card and took it home with me to show Keri. About six months later I gave a talk about grief and hope to more than five hundred people in a nearby city. After my talk, a woman approached me. "Your talk brought us comfort," she said. "My daughter lost her little girl earlier this year and we're both grateful for the hope you shared with us. She wanted to thank you but she's having a hard time."

I looked over to see a young woman looking toward us, her eyes swollen from crying. "I'll talk to her," I said.

I walked over to the young woman and for several moments held her while she cried. Then she said to me, "Mr. Evans, I've been to your angel statue in Salt Lake City."

At that moment I had a vision. I saw the Easter card I had taken home.

Without thinking, I said, "You left a card for your daughter that said you hoped there are Easter dresses where she is."

Both women stared at me in amazement. Then the young woman said, "How did you know that?"

"I just saw it," I said. "I had a vision."

The women left with a new sense of hope in the miracle we'd experienced together. This was a powerful reminder to me, not only of that experience but also of my belief that there is more to heaven and earth than is dreamt of in my philosophies. For me, there is something deeply reassuring about that.

AN ANSWERED PRAYER

The timing couldn't have been worse. Our family had just moved to Florence, Italy, when my five-year-old daughter, Abigail, complained of a toothache. In the States, this would have been a simple phone call and trip to our dentist. But here we didn't speak the language, know of a dentist, or even know where in the city to find one. In addition, we didn't know anyone we could turn to for help.

I found a phone book in one of the drawers in our apartment and looked up the word *dentista*.

I saw the name Leonardo Brunelleschi. I dialed the number.

"*Pronto.*"

"Do you speak English?" I asked.

There was a moment of hesitation, and then he said, "I speak the English."

"My daughter has a toothache. Can you see her today?"

"Today? Yes. You come at two o'clock in afternoon. *Ciao.*"

I wrote down the dentist's name and address, which was near a piazza, and that afternoon, with my daughter in pain, drove through the labyrinth of Florence's Etruscan-designed road system. I soon discovered that what I thought was the dentist's name was really the name of the piazza.

For nearly forty minutes, Abigail and I walked up and down the street looking for anything that resembled a dentist's office. There was nothing.

Finally, we stepped off the street into an alley. "I'm going to pray," I told Abigail. I said, "God, my little girl is in pain. I can't find this dentist. Please help us."

Simple prayer. Simple faith. Then we began walking the street again. After another fifteen minutes of searching we were nowhere closer. Finally I conceded defeat. As we walked back to our car I noticed a woman in the distance. She was more than a block away, standing on the sidewalk outside a building staring at me. To my surprise, she shouted, "Reeeeechard!"

How was this possible? I was in a strange country and literally knew no one. Not to mention that the woman was so far away. I probably wouldn't have recognized my own wife at that distance. Then I wondered if she was really calling to me, or if it was one of those experiences when someone waves at you and you wave back before realizing the person was waving at someone behind you. I turned around but there was no one around us. When I looked back, her gaze remained locked on me.

"Reeeechard," she shouted again. "Is it you?"

Taking Abigail's hand, I walked toward the woman. As we

neared, she said, "Yes, it is you, Richard. You have finally come to Italy."

I still had no idea who she was. As if anticipating my question, she pointed to herself and said, "It's me, Claudia."

"I'm sorry," I said. "How do I know you?"

"Do you not remember? I showed you an apartment." She was one of a half dozen apartment managers Keri and I had met six months earlier as we looked for a place to live. I had met her only once and briefly at that. "What are you doing in this place?" she asked.

"We're looking for a dentist."

"What is his name?"

"I don't know. I thought it was Leonardo Brunelleschi."

"That is the piazza name," she said.

"I know that now," I said. I showed her the paper I had written the address on.

"Hmm," she said. "I know this place. He is my dentist." She looked up. "I will show you to him."

We walked at least fifty yards off the road down a maze of alleys and streets. The sign for the dentist's office was only three inches long—all but invisible.

We thanked Claudia, and Abigail and I went upstairs to the dentist. I never saw Claudia again.

You could call it a coincidence, but that seems a little unlikely. Or a lot unlikely. I believe there is power in prayer. Sometimes there is divine intervention.

CRUCIFYING SANTA

Some years ago I read a newspaper article about a strange East-meets-West phenomenon. The Japanese had discovered Christmas and, aided by enterprising retailers, had taken the season to heart. Aware that the holiday had something to do with a bearded man in a red suit and the birth of Jesus Christ, they, not unlike the rest of us, didn't quite grasp the connection. It should have come as no surprise, then, when American tourists were horrified to encounter a Christmas display in a Tokyo department store window with a red-suited Santa Claus nailed to a cross.

While that story was revealed to be an urban legend, I'm afraid I've crucified a few Santas myself. As one who cherishes the season, I reluctantly confess to spending a good deal of my life oblivious to its deeper meaning—guilty of not seeing the forest for the Christmas trees. In defense of my ignorance, it is not difficult to be distracted by Yule tinsel, for Christmas is so often defined by its myriad symbols: stars, bells, wreaths, reindeer, baubles, bows, mistletoe, poinsettias, candles, and candy canes. But if you strip away the facade and symbols of the season, what remains?

It was in just such a circumstance that I truly found Christmas in a place where there ostensibly was no Christmas: the country of Taiwan, a world removed from Rudolphs and Grinches, church bells and manger scenes, far from friends and family, far from the streetlamp ornaments and garlands that overhung the snow-packed streets of home. Outwardly, there was no evidence of the season. None.

Yet among the golden temples, water buffalo, and rice paddies, Christmas was still there, deep inside my heart. And even though it made my heart burn with homesickness, my heart did burn. Brightly. And I was filled with love for the season and gratitude for all that I was missing: my family, my friends, my country. I was fortunate to have so much in my life to miss so badly.

In this state of heart, I came to the realization that it is, perhaps, not as much a question of what Christmas is about as it is what we are about. That is, while we are attempting to define the season, the season, in fact, is far more adept at defining us—asking our hearts to hear its call of love and joy and peace on earth, goodwill toward men.

WHY I DON'T THINK CHRISTMAS IS TOO COMMERCIAL

When I read the title of this essay to my immensely rational wife, she gave me *that* look—the one that says, *Are you completely insane?* To which I silently replied, *No, honey. Not completely.*

But as the *New York Times* has crowned me "the King of Christmas Fiction," I have a stake in this whole Christmas affair and I'm pretty sure I'm right about this. So please give me enough grace to hear me out.

Every holiday season, as predictable as eggnog and mistletoe, comes the familiar complaint that "Christmas is too commercialized."

Humbug. They're making commercialization sound like it's a bad thing. It's not. Not if you really think about it.

The general definition of *commercialization* is "to manage an activity or event in a way to make a profit." You mean, the way smart people manage charities and schools and hospitals—all worthwhile endeavors in my book. Profits are a good thing—even for "nonprofits." Profits assure survival and sustainability. (Harvard has a $53 billion endowment fund.) Without profits, businesses, products and productions, charities, churches, and organizations disappear. No worthwhile endeavor ever disappeared because it was too profitable. Never happened. Never will.

Before I became a full-time novelist, I was a copywriter at a small advertising agency. It was my job to commercialize things. I learned firsthand the veracity of the Ad Council's slogan, "A terrible thing happens without advertising. Nothing."

Nothing indeed. Just try to imagine a noncommercial Christmas. Begin by wiping out the Christmas decorations around your house and neighborhood that were created by people and companies with the hope of . . . wait for it . . . profit. That big plastic manger scene on your church lawn? Gone. Christmas tree lots? Nope, just bare asphalt. Those downtown Christmas decorations? Nonexistent. They were put up by the local chamber of commerce to attract crowds to the downtown shops and businesses because crowds bring shoppers and shoppers bring . . . profits.

But stay with me. What about the sounds and music of Christmas that evoke such joy? It's precisely because of the commercial value of Christmas that talented singers and songwriters—from Bing Crosby to Mariah Carey—have, no doubt with their agents' and record labels' nudges, created the Christmas music we enjoy. And it's also the reason radio stations play those songs for free, interwoven with a solid schedule of commercial advertising.

The Christmas movies? Yep, funded by investors hoping for a profit. So erase your *Grinch* and *Charlie Brown Christmas*, *It's a Wonderful Life* (which, initially, wasn't so profitable), and *A Christmas Carol*.

And books? Yep. There's profit there too. Dickens was in a personal financial crisis—a condition he hoped to alleviate—when he wrote the Yuletide classic *A Christmas Carol*.

For many businesses, the Christmas season is when they make the bulk of their profits, if not all of them. Hence the term "Black Friday"—the day US businesses go into the black of profitability. And a good thing happens when businesses make a lot of profits. In most cases the people behind those businesses start giving away money. Not just by spending more—which they do—and not just in salaries and Christmas bonuses but in charitable ways as well.

As the founder of a charitable organization, the Christmas Box International, I can attest that there is a direct correlation between profits and Americans' charitable giving—which is why, during the last recession, nearly a third of all the charities in America closed their doors.

So, is the cry against commercialization about the act of gift giving itself? Is it that the purchasing of material goods distracts from the "true" meaning of Christmas? My answer: Only if you let it. Yes, I'm as disgusted as you are by the avarice and violence of the Black Friday Walmart scenes that populate social media newsfeeds every holiday season. But let's be honest: those are a few incidents out of millions.

To me, the true meaning of Christmas is about a gift—the gift of God's redemption and hope. And what better way to celebrate this supernal endowment than to give gifts ourselves? Isn't that what the original Christmas celebrants—the wise men—showed us? And this is where the anti-commercialization folks are quick to quote the brilliant Emerson: "Rings and jewels are not gifts but apologies for gifts. The only true gift is a portion of thyself."

But let's roast this chestnut. Given that it's unlikely that Emerson was speaking literally, as though by gifting "a portion of thyself" he meant giving a finger or a kidney (the latter of which would no doubt make a very fine Christmas gift for someone in need), Emerson must have been referring to our time and attention, which, ironically, is exactly what was required of me to make the money to buy that gift I gave you.

As a child, I remember saving nickels and dimes I earned shoveling snow from the neighbors' walks to buy my brother a gift for Christmas—a *Mad* magazine paperback book. It cost $3.95, a veritable fortune, requiring that I save for months. And what joy that piece of commercialization brought both of us on Christmas morning and beyond. Fifty years later, my brother still has that book.

Without commercialization, Christmas would likely be more like Easter, memorialized with a few sermons and hymns in church, for those who go to church. There wouldn't be a

Christmas season; there would be a Christmas *moment*, forgotten as quickly as the week's sermon.

The truth is, too often people whine about the commercialization of Christmas because it makes the whiners feel morally superior to those materialistic hedonists they're hoping to elevate themselves above. But all this smugness is little more than pious self-aggrandizement and I have a strong suspicion that those "morally superior complainers" are the same people who decry Starbucks for not commercializing Christmas by plastering the word all over their paper coffee cups. Sorry, whiners, you can't drink your coffee and have it too.

The bottom line: I think it's those who complain loudest that Christmas is too commercial who are the ones with the problem of commercializing Christmas in their hearts. As for me, I don't feel it. The music and decorations and store window displays have all happily conspired to bring me fond memories of the season and Christmases past.

So bring on the nonstop Christmas carols and commercials, Christmas sales, Black Fridays, Cyber Mondays, and Giving Tuesdays. Deck the halls and streetlamps with foil and glitter. Sell us your peppermint-stick ice cream and chocolate orange balls and Elves on the Shelves and icicle Christmas lights, because all that glitter and glam is just a reflection of something much more beautiful and memorable—a communal celebration of family and joy and love and, yes, even the truest meaning of Christmas. And, in the paraphrased words of Scrooge's nephew Fred, all that Christmas cheer could do me no harm.

Is It Enough?

Christmas Night.

*As the evening falls
like the curtain on a
long-awaited show,*

*I hold my daughter
in the warm bath of the
Christmas tree lights.*

And I wonder.

*Did the Yuletide parties
and gatherings fill her
with a sense of family?*

*Did the Christmas rituals
unite her in a shared
commonality with
her fellow men?*

*Did the music of Christmas
heal her of a cynical world
and inspire her with hopes
of something greater?*

Did the gifts she shared
teach her that the greatest gifts
are received in the giving?

Did the once-wrapped
presents of Christmas remind
her of a greater gift given
many Christmases ago?

And I wonder.

Is there enough awe
in my child,
enough magic left,
to save a world?

For within my heart
I lament a great truth—

That the only promise of childhood
is that it will end.

And I wonder what
I have given her
to take its place.

And is it enough?

SHORT STORIES
AND FABLES

THE DANCE

A father once had a daughter. She was a happy little girl who liked the things that little girls do—dress-ups and kittens and sometimes both together. But most of all she liked to dance. Nearly every day she would jump and spin in the thick wild grass near the edge of the yard where the tall meadow flowers grew. Though she didn't see him, her father watched. And he smiled.

When the girl was old enough to go to school, she danced in the Thanksgiving play, dressed as an ear of corn. She could not see out of her costume very well and tripped over a boy dressed as a carrot. Though she could not see her father, he was watching. And he smiled.

When the girl was a little older, she took dancing lessons. She wore a pink tutu and soft leather ballet slippers. At her first dance recital she tried very hard to remember her steps. She did not see her father standing close to the stage. But he was smiling.

A few years later the girl became a graceful ballerina. She wore pink satin toe shoes with long shiny ribbons. One year she danced a solo in *The Nutcracker*. Everyone clapped when she finished. The crowd was large and the stage lights were bright so the girl could not see her father in the audience. But he clapped louder than anyone else. And he smiled wider than anyone else.

The girl grew into a young woman. One spring night she put on a beautiful gown and high-heeled pumps and went to her first prom with a young man. When the young man brought her home, they did not see her father peeking out the window as they slow-danced on the front porch. (He wasn't smiling.)

The young woman fell in love with the young man and they soon decided to marry. At the end of the wedding day, she waltzed with her father. Then the father gave his girl's hand to the young man and left the dance floor. As the young woman gazed into her new husband's eyes, she did not see her father watching from the side of the room. Though the father's eyes were moist, he smiled.

The young woman and her new husband moved far away from the home with the thick grass and tall meadow flowers. Whenever he missed his daughter, the father would take out an old shoebox filled with photographs of her dancing. As he looked at the pictures, he remembered each dance. And he smiled.

Many years passed. One day the father called his daughter on the telephone. "I am old now. I am cold and very tired," he said. "Please come to me. I would like to see you dance just one more time." The daughter came. She found her father in bed. And she danced for him. But the father did not smile. "I cannot see you," he said. "My eyes are not much good. Dance close to the bed so that I can hear your feet."

The woman walked close to the bed, then she jumped and spun as she had as a little girl. The father smiled. Then the woman sat on her father's bed. She lay her face against his, took his hand, and they swayed back and forth. In this way, they danced once more.

"I have danced many times," the woman whispered into her father's ear, "in many places and for many people. But I have always danced for you. How can I ever dance again?" She buried her head in her father's chest.

But her father shook his head. "You must never stop dancing," he said. "For though you will not see me, whenever you dance, I will be watching."

Then the father went to sleep. As the daughter sadly left his side, she stopped in the doorway and looked back at the father she loved. And then she danced. And though she could not see him, her father was watching. And he smiled.

THE SPYGLASS

A Fable about the Power of Faith

Once there was a great kingdom. This kingdom was known throughout all the lands for its splendor: its magnificent buildings, its great terraced gardens, and its bountiful farms. But through time, all that had changed. Now the once-great buildings were falling down and in need of much repair. The farms were now small and did not grow enough food for the kingdom. The poor villagers would oftentimes go to bed hungry.

The people of this kingdom were not just poor by way of things but also poor of spirit—for there was not much joy in the village. There were no dances around the maypole nor palace cotillions. Rarely was music heard but for the simple pluckings of the lute of a traveling minstrel now and again. Worst of all, the people had forgotten why their kingdom was once great.

The king of this land did not look as you might expect a king to look, for he did not have a magnificent throne or flowing robes or a golden crown inlaid with precious gems. He was the king of a poor kingdom, so he looked quite ordinary and poor himself. His castle was always cold and run-down. He had but one manservant and one milkmaid. He did not entertain the kings of other lands, for he was greatly ashamed of his kingdom.

To the east of this unhappy land was a beautiful kingdom with great farms and glorious cathedrals and castles. There were lovely gardens adorned with fine sculptures and sparkling fountains. Night and day, the breeze from the city walls carried the most exquisite music and the enticing scents of perfume—myrrh, cassia, and cypress—as well as the smell of delicacies, for there was an abundance of food in the land. It made the people even more unhappy to look on the wealth of their neighbors, for despite their poverty, the people prided themselves on having once been a great kingdom.

The king did not often leave his castle, for he was weary of the complaints of his subjects. One day as he sat down to a meager dinner of bread, a slab of cheese, and boiled mutton, there came a knock at the castle door. The king's servant opened the door to find an old man with a large oak walking stick. The man wore a cap and a girdle and a coarse woolen tunic. A large cloak of skins was draped over his shoulders. He was carrying a leather canister, which hung from his shoulder by rawhide thongs.

"Hail," said the old man. "I was but passing through your kingdom to the village to the east. I am looking for an inn to spend the night."

The servant frowned. "This is not an inn. This is the king's castle."

The traveler looked around in surprise. "This is not much of a castle," he said.

"Aye," the servant agreed.

"Still, I am weary from my journey. I would like to rest here."

"You must inquire of my lord," the servant said.

"Lead me to him," said the old man.

The servant led the old man down a dark, cold hallway to the king's dining room.

The king looked up from his meal as the man entered.

"You are the king of this land?" the old man asked.

"I am," the king replied.

"You do not look like a king."

The king frowned. "I am the king of a poor kingdom. Our farms yield no crops, our buildings are falling down, and my people weary me day and night with their complaints. We were once a great kingdom, but all that has changed."

The old man nodded slowly. "Why do you not change back?" he asked.

"Change?" the king replied angrily. "We have tried, only to fail. We lack all knowledge of what once made this kingdom great."

"You lack but one thing," said the old man. "If you will give me supper and lodging for the night, I will, on the morrow, show you why you fail."

The king looked at him thoughtfully, then said, motioning to the platters of bread, cheese, and meat, "Eat your fill."

The servant brought in a wooden platter and the old man ate with the king. When the old man had finished his meal, the servant led him to a room. That night as the king lay in his bed he wondered if the stranger had tricked him.

The next morning the old man came to the king in his throne room. "You have lived up to your part of the bargain. Now I will live up to mine. Follow me."

The king followed the old man to the castle balcony. There the old man brought out a long, round canister and pulled from it a brass tube with a sewn leather cover. A spyglass. He raised the spyglass to his eye and looked out over the land until a smile crossed his face. Then he handed the spyglass to the king. "Look thither."

The king looked through the glass. He could see great farms and gardens, magnificent castles and cathedrals. He lowered the spyglass and said impatiently, "I have seen the wonders of the neighboring kingdom. I hear far too much of them."

"You are mistaken," said the old man. "It is your own kingdom you see."

The king again raised the spyglass. This time he recognized the hills and glens of his own kingdom. But where there had been barren pasture there were now fields of grain stretching as far as the eye could see. His own people were in the fields, their wagons overflowing with their harvest.

"You are a wizard," said the king. "It is a trick of the glass."

"It is no trick," said the old man.

But when the king put down the glass, his kingdom looked the same as before.

"Nothing has changed."

"No," said the old man. "Change requires work. But one must first see before doing."

The king again raised the glass. "What greatness this kingdom holds!"

"You have seen what might be," said the old man. "Now go and make it so. After two harvests I will return for my spyglass."

The king, on horseback, went out into his kingdom. He rode until he came to the edge of a once-beautiful garden, now overrun with weeds and thistles. No one walked in the garden. There was neither the happy cries of playing children nor the pleased sighs of lovers. A group of villagers were standing outside its fence. Their children played at their feet in the dirty roadway.

"Why do you not use the garden?" the king asked them.

"It is not fit, sire," replied a woman.

"So it is not," agreed the king. "But it could be. Look." The king held out the spyglass. One by one the villagers looked through the tube at the garden. The weeds and thistles were gone and the lawns were lush and inviting. But when they set down the glass, the garden had returned to its overgrown state.

"It is an amusing device," said one man. "But of no use."

"No use indeed," the king said. "Behold, knave." And he went to the garden and began to pull the weeds up by his own hand. When the villagers saw what he was doing, they too began to pull up weeds until they had uncovered a large marble statue of an angel, its wings spread, its face looking toward heaven. The people stared at the statue in silent awe.

At length, the king mounted his horse. Before he left he said, "You have seen what might be. Now make it so."

The king rode farther down the road until he came to a farmer sitting on the ground threshing grain with a small flail.

"How goes it, man?" the king asked.

The weary farmer barely looked up. "Can't grow e'en enough to feed ourselves, sire," the farmer replied sadly. The king lifted the spyglass from his coat. "Come hither, good man. Behold your farm."

The farmer lifted the eyepiece to his eye and gasped. "It is sorcery."

"You have seen what might be," said the king. "Now make it so."

Farther down the road the king came to a crumbling cathedral. The roof had rotted and fallen in, and it was no longer safe to enter its arched doors. There were tents pitched outside, where a small congregation had gathered. The king rode his horse up to the tents. The friar who stood before the people stopped speaking at his approach.

All turned to see the king.

"Why do you meet in tents?" the king asked.

"Why, sire, our cathedral has fallen."

"Why have you not rebuilt it?"

The friar opened his arms to his congregation. "We are few in number and poor."

"Have you shown your congregation what could be?" the king asked.

The friar looked quizzically at the king. "And what might that be?"

"See for yourself," said the king, handing him the spyglass. The friar looked through it and saw a new cathedral, larger than the decaying building and more elaborate, adorned with beautiful sculptures of saints and cherubs. The friar stared in awe. "By the grace of God," he said, "I have seen a vision."

"You have seen what might be," said the king. "Now make it so."

Day by day the king went out until he had visited all the people of his kingdom and shown them what might be. Though there were those who would not look through the glass or who refused to believe what they saw, the greater part of the villagers looked with wonder and hope.

That same year there was a plentiful harvest and the farmers filled their wagons and barns with grain. But not just the farmers prospered. The wagon builders were busy building wagons to carry all the grain. The millers were busy milling the grain into flour. For the first time in as long as the villagers could remember, there was more than enough to eat. Music and dancing again filled the streets. Old buildings were repaired and new buildings rose, including the beginning of the most majestic cathedral in all the land.

As promised, two harvests later the old man returned to the kingdom. He almost did not recognize the castle, so greatly had it changed. The scarred wooden door he had once knocked on was new and intricately carved. Beautiful tapestries adorned the now-polished marble floors. The castle's once-cold chambers were warmed with heat and music, and the king was attended to by a bevy of servants and maids. The king, dressed in lavish robes of fur and silk, warmly welcomed the old man.

"My friend," he said, "I have awaited your return. Look what prosperity your spyglass has brought my people. Let us make merry and prepare a great feast in your honor!"

The old man smiled. "You have done well," he said. "But I cannot tarry. I have only come for my spyglass, then I will be on my way."

At this the king frowned. "In the two seasons since you blessed us with your arrival we have accumulated much treasure. In exchange for the spyglass, I will trade all the gold in the royal coffers, with men and wagons enough to carry it to wherever your destination."

"You have spoken wisely," said the old man, "for the gift of the spyglass is worth more than all the gold in all the royal coffers throughout the land. But keep your gold. You no longer need the spyglass."

"But there is still much to be done," pleaded the king.

"Yes," said the old man. "But you no longer need the spyglass. You can see without it."

"How is it possible?" asked the king.

"The spyglass only showed you what could be if you believed, for it was only faith that you and your people lacked."

The king shook his head in disbelief. "How can this be? Faith is foolishness."

"So says the fool," the old man said. "Faith is the beginning of all journeys. It is by faith that the seed is planted. It is by faith that the foundation is dug. It is by faith that each book is penned and each song written. Only with faith can we see that which is not but can be. The eye of faith is greater than the natural eye, for the natural eye sees only a portion of the truth. The eye of faith sees without bounds or limits."

"I had not supposed," the king said.

"That is why you once failed," said the old man. "Faith is why you now succeed."

He placed his hand on the king's shoulder and said with a smile, "You have seen what might be. Now go and make it so."

And though the old man and his spyglass were never again seen in the land, the kingdom continued to prosper and became once more the great kingdom of old. Yet, despite their abundance of food, their beautiful buildings, their lush gardens, and their majestic cathedrals, it was ever after said of that kingdom that their greatest treasure was their faith.

THE TOWER

A Fable about Humility

There was once a young man who desired to be great. But he did not know how to become great. So, he went to the oldest man in the small Chinese village where he lived, for all the villagers trusted the old man and considered him wise.

"What is it to be great?" the young man asked.

"To be great is to be looked up to," said the old man.

The young man considered his words. Then he went home and built himself a platform to stand on. He took his platform to the center of the village and stood on it. "Now everyone must look up to me."

But not everyone did. That afternoon, a very tall man walked by. "How's the weather down there?" he asked.

"I must build a taller platform," the young man said. He sawed off a bamboo pole and added longer legs to his platform. Now he could see the tops of the villagers' heads.

"Now I am greater than they," he said, looking down on the people. "They all must look up to me."

"Not I," said a small voice.

He glanced around. A little girl stared down at him from the window of a pagoda.

"This will not do," said the young man. "What I need is a tower. A tower higher than anything ever built in the village."

He went to work building his tower. He chopped down an entire forest of trees and dragged them to the top of a hill. He worked long and hard every day, from sunrise to late into the night. He did not have time for family or friends or sunset walks along the banks of the river. Whenever someone approached him, he said, "Do not bother me. I am building a tower." Eventually everyone stayed away.

After many seasons the young man finished his tower. It stretched high into the air, high above the village. It was taller than the Dragon and Tiger Pagodas, higher even than the emperor's palace in the land to the north. The young man was tired, but he was pleased with his tower. "Now everyone must look up to me," he said. "I am the greatest man in the land."

There was room for only one at the top of his tower, and the young man soon found that he was lonely. But he told himself that it did not matter, for a great man must often walk alone. Besides, he reasoned, why would he want to associate with those so much lower than himself?

One day a bird flying by saw the young man on top of the tower. It flew down and alit on his knee. "What are you doing up here?" the bird asked.

Normally the young man would have sent away such a

common bird, but today he was feeling especially lonely and welcomed its company. "I am a great man," he said.

"Is that so?" said the bird. "A great man is an uncommon and good thing. I have always wanted to see a great man. Let me take a look at you."

The bird flew around the man. Then it again landed on the young man's knee.

"Excuse me for saying so, but I do not see anything about you that is so different from any other man. What makes you great?"

The young man smiled smugly. He did not expect a bird to know such things as what makes a man great. "Let me explain," he said. "I am much higher than everyone else. All must look up to me." He pointed to the people in the village below. "See how small they are from here."

"It would appear so," said the bird. "But then, perhaps, from the ground, you appear small to them."

For a moment the man was perplexed by the bird's observation. Then he said, "No matter. I am above them all. While they crawl with the animals and work their low fields, I sit high above them in the clouds."

"You are high indeed," said the bird. "It is a long way to fall."

"I will not fall," said the man. "My tower is strong, the likes of which has never been seen in this kingdom."

"All towers fall," said the bird, "with time."

The man ignored the bird's warning. He thought himself much too great to heed a common bird.

"You may be as great as you say," said the bird, "but I know of one who is greater."

The man cast his eyes about. "Where is this person?"

"She is an old woman. She is far below. She could never climb such a tower," said the bird, "but even we birds look up to her."

An arrogant grin crossed the man's face. "I have caught you in foolishness. If she is down below, how can she be looked up to?"

"I cannot explain it, but it is true," said the bird.

This angered the young man. "Where will I find this woman?"

"Where the river is at its widest, there is a large rock just right for sitting upon. At sunrise you will find her there." With that the bird flew away.

The bird's words bothered the man. He decided that he must see this woman for himself. The next morning, before the sun rose above the eastern mountains, he climbed down from his tower. At sunrise, he found the woman where the bird said she would be. To his surprise she was a very small woman, old and withered. Her clothes were ragged and poor. Still, she was surrounded by a flock of birds, for she took from her own loaf of bread and fed them.

"I have heard that you are great," the man said to the old woman.

The old woman looked up but did not reply. She broke off another piece of bread and threw it to the ground.

"You cannot be great," said the man. "No one looks up to you . . . except these little birds."

"No matter," the old woman replied.

The man puffed out his chest. "What do you know of the great man in the tower? You know of him, of course."

"All know of him," said the woman. "Whether he be great, I know not. He is nothing to me. But I pity him."

"Pity!" cried the man. "How can you pity a man whom all look up to?"

"I pity him because I think he must be miserable. He spends his life where it is cold and friendless. It is my experience that those who build such towers do not enjoy the climb or the height but only enjoy being higher than another. Such people must always be lonely."

The man replied tersely, "It is a small price to pay for being great."

"How do you know that the man is great?" she asked.

"Because all can see him and that makes him great."

"Being seen and being great are not the same thing."

"I don't understand," said the man.

"To be great," said the woman, "is not to be seen by others but to truly see others."

The woman threw the last of her bread to the birds, then turned and faced the man. "To be great is not to be higher than another but to lift another higher."

The man thought long and hard about this. "You speak strange things."

"Perhaps. But I am too old to lie."

The man turned and started walking back to his tower. As he walked, he came to a group of children playing. From his tower he could not hear the laughter of children, so he stopped to listen to it. Then he noticed a little boy sitting on the branch of a tree, apart from the others. The boy looked sad.

"Why are you not playing with the others?" the man asked.

"I would rather sit above them in this tree," he replied.

"But why?"

"Because it is better to be above them." He pointed toward the man's tower.

"Someday I will build a tower like the one on the hill. Then I will be happy."

"No," said the man as he turned to leave, "you will not be happy then."

The young man walked slowly back to his tower and looked at it for a long time. It stretched high up to the cold and lonely clouds. He thought about the old woman and the things she had said. And he thought about the little boy in the tree.

Then he took an axe and began to chop at the legs of the tower. To his surprise, the tower fell easily with a mighty crash. Then the young man sat down on a rock to think.

A villager was walking by and stopped to look at the man and the large pile of tangled wood behind him. "I am newly married and hope to build my wife a house. I could use some wood," he said.

"Help yourself," the young man said.

The new husband began to gather the wood.

"Do you need some help building?" the young man asked. "I have gotten good at building."

The husband smiled. "Thank you. I could use some help."

Word of the fallen tower spread throughout the village. There were many in need of wood, and the man shared freely of his tower with all who asked, turning no one away. Some used the wood to build fires to warm themselves and their families. Some made beautiful furniture and carvings. The young man even helped a group build a school in the center of the village. The whole village was changed by his gift.

As the man delivered up the last of his wood, he overheard one villager say to another, "Look how freely this man gives. You know what they say of him?"

"What is that?" asked the other.

"It is said that here is a truly great man."

THE LITTLE COW

A Brazilian friend of mine told me an old folktale called "The Little Cow." Admittedly in today's culture, the story comes off as a little shocking, but the moral of the story is still powerful. It went something like this.

A Master of Wisdom was walking through the countryside with his apprentice when they came to a small, disheveled hovel on a meager piece of farmland. "See this poor family," said the master. "Go see if they will share with us their food."

"But we have plenty," said the apprentice.

"Just do as I say," the master replied.

The obedient apprentice went to the home. The good farmer and his wife, surrounded by their seven children, came to the door. Their clothes were dirty and in tatters.

"Fair greetings," said the apprentice. "My master and I are sojourners and want for food. I've come to see if you have any to share."

The farmer said, "We have little, but what we have we will share." He walked away, then returned with a small piece of cheese and a crust of bread. "I am sorry, but we don't have much."

The apprentice did not want to take their food but did as he had been instructed. "Thank you. Your sacrifice is great."

"Life is difficult," the farmer said, "but we get by. And in spite of our poverty, we do have one great blessing."

"What blessing is that?" asked the apprentice.

"We have a little cow. She provides us milk and cheese, which we eat or sell in the marketplace. It is not much but she provides enough for us to live on."

The apprentice went back to his master with the meager rations and reported what he had learned about the farmer's plight. The Master of Wisdom said, "I am pleased to learn of their generosity, but I am greatly sorrowed by their circumstance. Before we leave this place, I have one more task for you."

"Speak, master."

"Return to the hovel and bring back their cow." The apprentice did not know why, but he knew his master to be merciful and wise, so he did as he was told. When he returned with the cow, he said to his master, "I have done as you commanded. Now what is it that you would do with this cow?"

"See yonder cliffs? Take the cow to the highest crest and push her over."

The apprentice was shocked. "Why would we do such a thing?"

"Just do as I say."

The apprentice sorrowfully obeyed. When he had completed the task, the master and his apprentice went on their way.

Over the next years, the apprentice grew in mercy and wisdom. But every time he thought back on the visit to the poor farmer's family, he felt a pang of guilt. One day he decided to go back to the farmer and apologize for what he had done. But when he arrived at the farm, the small hovel was gone. In its place was a large, fenced villa.

"Oh, no!" he cried. "The poor family who was here was driven out by my evil deed." Determined to learn what had become of the family, he went to the villa and pounded on its great door. The door was answered by a servant. "I would like to speak to the master of the house," he said.

"As you wish," said the servant. A moment later the apprentice was greeted by a smiling, well-dressed man.

"How may I serve you?" the master asked.

"Pardon me, sir, but could you tell me what has become of the family who once lived on this land but is no more?"

"I do not know what you speak of," the master replied. "My family has lived on this land for three generations."

The apprentice looked at him quizzically. "Many years ago, I walked through this valley, where I met a farmer, his wife, and their seven children. But they were very poor and lived in a small hovel."

"Oh," the man said, smiling, "that was my family. But my children have all grown now and have their own estates."

The apprentice was astonished. "But you are no longer poor. What happened?"

"God works in mysterious ways," the man said. "We had this little cow that provided us with the barest of necessities—enough to survive but little more. We suffered but expected no more from life. Then, one day, our little cow wandered off and fell over a cliff. We knew we would be ruined without her, so we did everything we could to survive. Only then did we discover that we had greater power and abilities than we possibly imagined, gifts we never would have found as long as we relied on that cow. What a great blessing from heaven to have lost our little cow."

In modern business vernacular that ancient concept has been translated to "good is the enemy of great." Life requires that we let go of the rung we cling to in order to climb higher. But we humans are naturally averse to change, and rarely change seats unless the seats become too painful to bear. We must let go of the past to reach the future. We can spend our days bemoaning our losses, or we can grow from them. Ultimately the choice is ours. We can be victims of circumstance or masters of our own fate, but make no mistake: we cannot be both.

A CONVERSATION
WITH THE REAPER

H e came like a thief in the night. I woke with a start from my troubled slumber at the sound of his intrusion—a slow shuffle outside my bedroom door. Fearfully, I pressed myself against the door as I imagined the specter lurking on the other side—a shadow cloaked in a black robe of linen, a faceless hood gaping dark and deep as a throat.

Then came the cold rapping of knuckles against my door. With my faltering strength I braced myself against it to keep him from entering.

"What do you want?" I asked.

His voice came arid as a desert wind. "I do not answer any question for which the answer is already known, my friend."

"You call me 'friend'?" I said bitterly.

"I'll call you what you wish," he replied. "What mortal name you pin to yourself matters not—nor changes my evening's errand."

"Then you are coming for me?"

He did not reply.

"Do not call me friend," I said. "I didn't invite you, nor do I welcome you."

"But you did invite me."

"When did I invite you?"

"The day you were born, our meeting was agreed upon. It was part of the accord."

"But I wasn't expecting you."

"How foolish," he replied, "to not expect the inevitable. Are you surprised by a sunset?"

"I wasn't expecting you right now."

"I am rarely expected," he said. "But I need no appointment. I can come at any time. Ask the winds that blow which leaf will be the next to fall. But, in turn, all must fall. It is the way of the tree. It is the way of all life."

"I have no desire to see you."

I heard what sounded like a sigh. "You make me feel unwelcome, friend. Not all turn me away. Often, the old and lonely and miserable seek me out. In time, if you had more time, even you would hope for my arrival. But you disappoint me, friend. How is it that you have not learned to receive me, nor other lessons of life?"

"I have learned of life," I said, "but not of death."

"Then you have learned of neither," came the voice. "For life can be understood only through death. How often is it said by humans that it is only after brushing against me that they came to know life? It is a cliché, is it not?"

I didn't answer.

"There is much you do not know," he said. "But sometimes I am patient, and tonight I have time, so ask me what you will. I will answer honestly, for I am the most honest of guests."

"If you're honest, why are you cloaked? And why do you conceal your face?"

"I conceal nothing. You are the tailor of the cloak I wear, not I. It is humanity that hides me. In truth I am naked and seen everywhere."

"Then tell me, cruel visitor, why do I fear you so?"

"Cruel? How you insult me. But still I will answer. You fear me, in part, because all humanity fears the unknown. But that is only part of the truth. It is not because you do not know me but because you do not know yourself. If you knew who you really are, you would know who I really am."

"And who is that?"

"I am the usher, not the destination."

I considered his words. "I still fear you."

"Is it because I pry your grip from the trifles to which you cling? Is it because I force open your eyes to the illusion of possession, even to your own mortality? Have you lived your life as the fools who spend their time acquiring what they must leave behind? For life was not meant to gather but to become."

"I should have known this sooner," I said. "I'm not ready for you."

"Alas, too often I hear that refrain, but it is wasted breath, for I, my friend, am ready for you."

Despite my efforts, the door began to open. I fell back onto my bed and shielded my eyes from my horrible caller.

"Look upon me," he said with power. "Remove the cloak from your mind and see me for who I truly am and know yourself."

Slowly I looked up. My visitor looked different than I had imagined. He wore not a black robe but a vibrant robe of green. His face was fair and comely, and his hands were not the chalk of bone but of flesh and supple and covered with rings. In his eyes was truth and I knew that all he had said was true. He smiled at me. "Yes, you remember now. I am the bearer of new life. Every beginning springs from another beginning's end. It is the greatest of all human truths, that death gives birth to life anew."

"I will come with you," I said.

"Yes, but only for a short while, for I come only to escort you to a new door. The journey is yours alone. I am not the destination."

THE
AUTHOR'S WORLD

ELVIS'S TOENAILS

My publicist and I arrived at the television station around 6 a.m. for an appearance on the morning news. I was there to plug my latest novel and my book signing that night in downtown Atlanta. After waiting in the greenroom for a few minutes, we were greeted by the show's producer, who informed us that there had been a scheduling mishap and that I wasn't on the show that morning but the next day.

My publicist went ballistic. "It's right here," she said, shaking my paper schedule a few inches from the producer's face. "He's supposed to be on your show this morning."

"I'm sorry," the producer said. "There was some kind of mistake. We have him scheduled for tomorrow."

"What good is tomorrow?" my publicist spat. "His book signing is tonight."

"I'm really sorry, but my hands are tied. Every segment is booked."

For the next few minutes, my publicist continued pressing my case without success. Finally, I intervened.

"If there's no room on the show, there's no room," I said. "I'll make you a deal. If you'll announce my book signing during your news, I'll come back tomorrow and do your show."

The producer happily agreed to the compromise.

The next morning I arrived on time at the TV station. As one of the studio crew clipped a microphone to my lapel, he said to me, "Do you know why you were bumped yesterday?"

I just looked at him. "I wasn't bumped," I said. "There was a scheduling mix-up."

"No, you were bumped. Do you want to know for who?"

"I guess."

"We had a woman on the show who was Elvis's pedicurist. And she brought a jar of Elvis's toenails."

"You bumped me for a jar of Elvis's toenails?"

"Yep," he said. "Have a good show."

TAKE THE SEAT

Since I began writing, I've written more than forty-five books. But it all started back in 1992, with a holiday novella I wrote called *The Christmas Box*.

After that little book, about the love of a parent for a child, was rejected by every publisher I sent it to, I decided to self-publish it. I didn't know anything about the industry, so I had no idea how difficult this would be. Back then there was no Amazon, no print-on-demand, no e-books. The only large bookstore chains were the Waldenbooks in the malls and the emerging Barnes & Noble bookstores. The book industry was primarily run through thousands of small, independent mom-and-pop bookstores.

Those were exciting days. But they were also challenging times for a self-published author. Without a central means to sell a book, it meant having to reach out to thousands of bookstore owners, something beyond the scope of most authors. It certainly was for me.

Still, I decided to try. To reach bookstore owners, I went to bookseller conferences where I could meet hundreds of booksellers at once. One of these conferences was the Mountains & Plains Independent Booksellers show in Denver, Colorado.

I set up my one-table booth, then stood behind the table waiting for people with the red badges, denoting them as booksellers. By noon on the first day I had met only a dozen booksellers. I was worried. The booth had cost me several hundred dollars, which was a lot of money for me back then. Finally, I went to one of the show's organizers to ask where all the booksellers were.

"They're in the other hall with the authors," she said.

"There's another hall?" I replied.

"Hall B," she said. "Where we hold the events."

I walked over to Hall B. As the woman said, there were hundreds of booksellers. There was a dais at the front of the hall with a row of tables with famous, bestselling authors like Mary Higgins Clark and John Grisham.

The booksellers waited in stanchioned lines for their turn to not only meet these famous authors but get free autographed copies of their upcoming books.

This is where I need to be, I thought. *These are the people I need to meet to sell my book.* The dilemma was, you had to be a bestselling author to be on that stage. And the way I saw it, I'd never be a bestselling author unless I got up there. Catch-22.

As I stood there looking enviously at the authors, I realized that there was an empty seat at one of the tables. *Want to be a bestselling author?* my inner voice said. *Take the seat.*

Yeah, right. There was no way I was going to just walk up

there and sit down between famous authors. I would be thrown out. There were "guards" up there.

Crestfallen, I started back to my booth. As I walked, my inner voice said, *How much do you care about your dreams? You want to be a successful author? Take the seat.*

Before I could talk myself out of it, I went back to my booth, grabbed a box of my books, and walked back to the hall. I walked around the big crowd and through the curtain, and sat down at the table with my books.

Someone noticed. Out of the corner of my eye I could see a woman walking toward me. *This is going to be humiliating*, I thought. But, as they say, fortune favors the bold. When she got to me I looked up at her and said, "Sorry I'm late."

Her expression changed from indignation to confusion. She hesitated for a moment, then said, "Would you like some water?"

That afternoon I got my little book into the hands of hundreds of booksellers.

The next year, *The Christmas Box* was one of the bestselling books in America. My new publisher had paid millions for the chance to publish my book, and I was invited to shows all across the nation, including the Mountains & Plains Independent Booksellers show in Colorado. Only this time I wasn't crashing the party. I was on the cover of the program and traveling with a small entourage.

The authors' meeting was held in the exact same hall as the year before. There was a little table tent with my name on it, and the other authors asked for my autograph. And, remarkably, the same woman was there from the year before. As she walked up to me I said to her, "Do you know who I am?"

RICHARD PAUL EVANS

She replied, "Yes, Mr. Evans, everyone here knows who you are. Your book is very popular."

"That's not what I meant," I said. "Do you remember me from last year?"

Her brow furrowed. "You weren't here last year." Then, as she looked at me, she said, "Wait. You're the guy who crashed the book signing!"

I grinned. "That was me."

"Congratulations, you did it."

"Thanks for not throwing me out," I said.

"I was going to, but when you looked up at me I couldn't do it," she said, smiling. "Would you like some water?"

THE MAN IN THE BUSH

I t was a warm summer day. I was driving to my mother-in-law's home in a small gated community when I noticed a pair of legs sticking up out of a bush. I stopped my car and rolled down the window.

"Hey. You in the bush. Are you okay?"

"Yep," came an elderly man's voice.

"Do you need some help?"

"I'd sure appreciate it." Upside down, the man was wearing compression stockings, loafers, and polyester pants. I grabbed him by his arms and, with some exertion, pulled him out of the bush.

After he was out and standing fairly steadily, I asked, "How did you fall in a bush?"

"I don't really know. I was just walking. Next thing I know, I'm in a bush."

"Did you call for help?"

"No. My son was coming by later today so I figured he would probably see me."

I walked the man about fifty yards back to his house. His wife was sitting at the kitchen table drinking coffee over a crossword puzzle as we walked in.

"Your husband fell in a bush," I said. "He's not hurt."

The woman just stared at me for a moment, then she said to her husband, "You brought home Richard Paul Evans?"

He looked at me and then back at her and said, "Who?"

"Richard Paul Evans. He's an author. I have all his books."

"I don't know who he is. He pulled me out of a bush."

She looked back at me and said, "Thanks for bringing him home, Richard. As long as you're here, would you mind signing a few books?"

FAMOUS

At one of my early book signings, I was seated at a table in front of a bookstore in a crowded mall when a man walked up to me. He looked at my book, then back at me.

"Are you famous?"

"Have you ever heard of me?" I replied.

He looked at my name on my poster. "Nope."

"Then I'm not famous."

"Oh." He walked away.

This is the acid test: If you have to tell someone you're famous . . . you're not.

HOW TO SLIT THROATS
(AND OTHER USEFUL
THINGS AUTHORS
SHOULD KNOW)

I was on one of the myriad flights of my book tour, sitting in the window seat of a crowded commuter plane. In stagnant moments like that I try to catch up on the more mechanical parts of my writing, particularly research. I had twenty minutes before takeoff and a friend had given me the phone number of an emergency room doctor to answer a few questions I had for the book I was writing at the time, *The Last Promise*. There's a part where (spoiler alert) a man is falsely accused and imprisoned for murder. The research I needed was for the somewhat grisly but necessary backstory of the murder scene.

I took out my notepad and pencil, then called the

doctor. Surprisingly, he was available to talk. This is what the conversation sounded like from my end.

"Hi, this is Richard Paul Evans . . . Yes . . . Thank you for taking my call. I just have a few quick questions. Thank you. My question is, if I wanted to kill someone with a knife, and I wanted to be sure that they died but not have their death be immediate, where would be the best place to cut them? . . .

"Let me write that down . . . the carotid artery . . . both sides of the neck. About where you would take a pulse. Okay, I know where that is. How deep would the blade need to go? . . . Okay. And you think they'll last how long? . . . Would they still be able to scream? . . . Perfect. That's all I need to know. Thank you so much for your time. You've been very helpful. I'll let you know how it turns out."

I hung up my phone, turned it off, and put it in my pocket. I looked over my notes, then put my notebook in the seat pouch and sat back, fastening my seat belt. That's when I noticed the man sitting next to me. He looked pale. He was looking straight ahead, pretending he hadn't heard anything.

"Sorry about that," I said.

"No worries," he said, his voice trembling. "I didn't hear anything."

I went back to writing. A moment later the man turned to me and asked, "Are you a lawyer?"

PECULIAR COINCIDENCES IN BOOK WORLD

I was sequestered away in the small southern Utah town of St. George working on my third book, a historical novel called *The Letter*. Those were pre-Google days, and sometimes I would hire multiple researchers to discover even the most seemingly inconsequential detail, like the 1812 Grass Valley train schedule. The book I was working on takes place during the Depression, and I needed information on Franklin D. Roosevelt's Civilian Conservation Corps, better known as the CCC. I went to the town's small library but couldn't find anything on the subject.

Henry David Thoreau once said that our feet are connected to our brains. Like Thoreau, I walk for inspiration, and I was happy to learn that the city of St. George had recently constructed a new walking trail that went all the way to the neighboring suburb of Bloomington.

I was walking along the trail lost in my thoughts when

I heard a bicycle bell. *When was the last time I heard one of those?* I thought.

I turned around to see an old man riding a bike that looked nearly as old as he was. It had a plastic wicker basket, a flag, and a handlebar bell.

He pulled his bike up alongside me and slowed to my pace. "Good afternoon, young man," he said. "Nice day for a walk."

"Really nice," I said. "This is a nice walking path."

"Yes, it is," he said. "It reminds me of the trails we used to build for the CCC."

I could hardly believe it. "You worked for the CCC?"

"Oh yeah. For five years."

"Tell me about it."

He spent the next half hour telling me everything I needed to know about the CCC and his experience. When he finished telling me what he knew, he smiled and said, "I've talked your ear off. Have a good day." He rang his bell and rode off.

What are the odds? I thought. I walked back to my hotel room and wrote.

THE HOLOCAUST
SURVIVOR

There have been times in my life and career that I have experienced remarkable and unlikely coincidences. Returning to America from a book tour in Poland was one of those times.

I have a loyal following in Poland, and, to my delight, my Polish publisher arranged to have me tour the country. (I had always wanted to eat a real pierogi.) I was kept busy with media and book signings and didn't have the chance to visit some of the sites I had hoped to see. One of those sites was the Sobibor extermination camp. I had especially wanted to see Sobibor as I had made a character in one of my book series—*The Walk*—a survivor of the camp.

There weren't many survivors. Sobibor was created with one despicable purpose—to kill Jewish people as efficiently as possible.

Sobibor was also one of the few camps where the prisoners had attempted an uprising, and some three hundred prisoners escaped, though, in the days following the revolt, most of them were hunted down and executed. Of the nearly 250,000 Jewish people interned at Sobibor, only fifty-eight are believed to have survived.

The character in my book was a Holocaust survivor named Leszek. After much research, I based him on one of those escapees from Sobibor, specifically on one of two brothers who had escaped and been hidden from the Germans by a sympathetic Polish farmer.

As I waited for my flight home in the Warsaw airport, I saw a dozen or so Jewish men and women dressed in Orthodox clothing. I noticed that their activity seemed to revolve around an older man with a thick gray beard. I guessed that the man was perhaps a rabbi or someone else of importance in the Jewish community.

After I boarded the flight, the elderly man was escorted onto the plane and, to my surprise, was seated next to me. The men helping him were speaking a language I didn't know, so after they left, I smiled at the man, but we never spoke.

The flight from Warsaw to Miami took a little over eleven hours and the elderly man slept for most of the flight. He was sleeping when the pilot announced our approach into Miami International Airport and the flight attendants came down the aisles checking the passengers' seat belts. When an attendant woke my companion, he seemed a little confused, as if unsure of what the attendant was asking him to do.

"I'll help him," I said. I reached over and buckled his seat belt for him. He nodded a thank you, then looked ahead.

A moment later he turned back to me and said in perfect English, "Are you Polish?"

I was surprised to hear him speak English. "No. I'm American."

"So am I. Why were you in Poland?"

"I'm an author," I said. "I was on a book tour."

"You're an author," he said. "How interesting. What kind of books do you write?"

"Novels," I replied. "Inspirational novels."

"You should write my story," he said.

"Do you have a good story?"

"I don't know if it's good, but it would be interesting to read."

"Why were you in Poland?" I asked.

"I came with a group from our synagogue," he said. "I am a Holocaust survivor. Sixty-five years ago I was carried out of Auschwitz by a Russian soldier. I was just days away from dying from hunger. I had made myself a promise that before I died, I would walk out of the camp on my own feet."

"Were you in Auschwitz the whole war?"

"No. I was moved through several camps."

"Did you know of a concentration camp called Sobibor?"

His expression turned gray at the mention of the place. He slowly shook his head and said softly, "Sobibor. What a horrible place, Sobibor."

"Did you ever go to Sobibor?"

His heavy brow fell. "No. No one left Sobibor." He again shook his head, then said, "That's not completely true. There was a revolt in Sobibor. There were a few who escaped. Very few." He looked me in the eyes. "One of them was my cousin."

"Your cousin escaped?"

"Yes. He and his brother escaped. His brother did not make it. My cousin was saved by a poor Polish farmer."

Incredibly, the man I had based my character on was his cousin.

I told him what a remarkable coincidence meeting him was, and that I had based a character in one of my books on his relative. He flashed a big smile, then told me that after the war his cousin immigrated to America and became a successful Florida real estate developer. One of the first things he did with his wealth was go back to Poland to help the poor farmer who had risked his life to save his.

"That poor farmer now owns a very large farm," my new friend said. "With tractors and trucks and all kinds of machinery."

"I like stories like that," I said. "And yours."

"You should write my story," he said again.

I thought for a moment, then answered honestly, "I'm not sure I could do it justice. I think you should write your story. I'd love to hear it from your perspective. I think a lot of people would."

He smiled at me and said, "Maybe I will someday. Maybe I will."

It's been years since that meeting. I've lost track of him. I don't even know if he's still alive. But I have no doubt that I was meant to meet him. The odds that we were in Poland at the same time are astronomical. Even more that we were on the same flight and sitting next to each other.

I don't believe it was a coincidence. I believe it was a

God thing. While for some the mathematics of the universe suggests the existence of a Supreme Being, to me, it is that which defies math's probabilities that gives the most evidence of God—the improbability of two objects colliding in an infinite void. In this, God, not the devil, is in the details.

THE EXTRAORDINARY
POWER OF AN IDEA

O n July 16, 1945, at an army testing site in the desert near Alamogordo, New Mexico, the first atomic bomb was detonated. No one who gathered that day to witness the blast was sure what would happen. In fact, there was a pool among scientists about how big the explosion would be. There was an outside chance, surmised one scientist, that the bomb would set off a nuclear reaction that would destroy the entire universe.

While the universe was spared, the explosion was enormous, its energy equivalent to that released by forty million pounds of dynamite—equal to all the energy produced and consumed in the United States every thirty seconds—that's every car, lamp, dishwasher, diesel engine, airplane, train, factory, everything. However, this bomb's energy was released in a few millionths of a second, and in a volume only a few inches wide.

The resulting explosion was terrible. The hundred-foot

steel tower on which the bomb was mounted was completely vaporized. The ball of air formed by the explosion boiled up to a height of thirty-five thousand feet, higher than Mount Everest. For hundreds of yards around the blast site the surface of the desert sand was turned to glass.

Yet the atom that started the explosion was so small that for millennia man didn't know it even existed. It was so small that a million of them lined end to end would be roughly the width of a human hair. How could something that small create so much power?

The atom is the perfect metaphor for an idea. Like the atom, the infinitesimally small spark of an idea can start a chain reaction that can change the world.

It is amazing to me that the American Revolution, the Pyramids, World War II, Democracy, the Great Wall of China—all these major events or creations began in one mind with one idea. Like atoms, these ideas interacted with others and set off a chain reaction that grew in force until it was unstoppable.

Oliver Wendell Holmes Sr. wrote, "Man's mind, once stretched by a new idea, never regains its original dimensions." If you want to understand just how true this statement is, just think of the impact of Darwin's theory of evolution, Freud's concept of the unconscious, or Einstein's theory of relativity.

I keep a notebook of ideas. You never know when something world-changing might come along.

HANGING WITH
THE BUSHES

W hen I was twelve years old, my grandfather gave me a blessing. In it he said that I would someday walk with the royalty of this earth and be known throughout the world as one who loved God. This, I believe, is a literal manifestation of that blessing to a poor little boy.

In 2005, I was invited by the late Barbara Bush to speak at her literacy event in Texas. Prior to the event, the speakers, four of us, had lunch at the Bush residence in Houston. The experience was a bit surreal, sitting around the table talking to former president George H. W. Bush about his new exercise pool and being interrupted by a call from comedian Dana Carvey, who was still working on his "thousand points of light" imitation.

The other speakers that day were *Time*'s Hugh Sidey and former British prime minister John Major. Mrs. Bush informed us that the fourth scheduled guest, Reba McEntire, was ill and would not be joining us, but she had found a "surprise" replacement. That afternoon as we settled in at the conference center for the mic check, the surprise visitor arrived—their son, George W. Bush, the current president.

I was sitting by myself in the still-empty auditorium when the president walked out to meet me. We shook hands and he began to tell me a joke about a duck. I never heard the punch line because Mrs. Bush, looking down from the stage, suddenly shouted, "George! Just leave the author alone!" The president turned to me and said, "I'm the leader of the free world, and my mother still tells me what to do."

The next day, we were given a private tour of the George H. W. Bush Presidential Library & Museum. As it turned out, Mrs. Bush and I ended up alone together for the ride back to my hotel in a black armored SUV driven by the Secret Service. As we made the trip, Mrs. Bush sat next to me quietly knitting, something I noticed she did a lot of. I said to her, "I think it's amazing that the Bush family has created an American dynasty without being blue bloods." Mrs. Bush looked up at me with an almost shocked expression. "Richard," she said, "our blood is bluer than you think."

Hanging on my office wall is a copy of a letter the late George H. W. Bush sent me after reading one of my books.

RANDOM MUSINGS

WHAT DOES LOVE REQUIRE?

We live in angry times. People are anxious and afraid, which makes them act angrily. We see people in public places lashing out, insulting, shaming, shoving, even spitting on other people. We see road rage on highways and fistfights on airplanes. But all this anger is, perhaps, most evident on social media. Behind social media's curtain, people act in ways they would never have the courage, or at least the foolishness, to act in person. Trolls abound.

In this heightened environment of fear and anger, it is even more important that we do one of the hardest things we humans can do—return good for evil. It's not easy. But it is powerful. And it is truly good. I have seen its effect.

Many years ago I received an angry email from a woman in Scotland. The woman had heard that my first book, *The Christmas Box*, was healing for people who had lost children. She ordered the book, only to discover that she had ordered the wrong one. Instead, she had purchased *The Christmas Box Miracle*, a nonfiction book I wrote about the miraculous way that first book had come to me and the miracles and healing I'd seen come from it.

The woman was surprisingly angry. Even though I had never had any sort of contact with her, she blamed me for the deception that had confused her and "stolen" her money. She called me a hypocrite and wrote that I pretended to be a good person when I was nothing more than a crook. She added that I was cruel and greedy to make money off my mother's loss of a baby. She wrote that she too had lost a child and, as such, I made her sick.

Now I was angry. This woman not only blamed me for the mistake she made but then took it to a ridiculous level of calumny. Her message was full of misspellings and grammatical errors. She was an easy target.

I wrote back that she was one of the nastiest, most pathetic people I'd come across in my career and that it was clear from her writing that she was obviously of below-average intelligence, so it wasn't surprising that she ordered the wrong book. I told her how sad it was that there are small-minded, nasty people like her in this world.

Then, as I looked over my written attack, my heart hurt. Was this *really* who I was or wanted to be? Was my attack really any different from hers? Sure, she'd drawn first blood, but, at its core, wasn't my intent the same as hers—to injure and hurt someone else? It was then that I noticed, truly noticed, the understated line about her losing a child. What pain she must have been in. It's natural for people in pain to lash out. I erased my email. Then I wrote a very different one.

I wrote that I was sorry she had been confused by the books' titles, that it wasn't my or my publisher's intent to deceive, and that I would send her, free of charge, one of the original books if she still wanted it. I wrote that I loved my mother and that my mother was my book's biggest fan—that it had not only eased her pain but also brought her joy that others were comforted through her loss. I told this woman that I couldn't imagine the heartbreak she had gone through in losing a child and how truly sorry I was for her loss. I again asked her forgiveness for the book confusion and wished her well.

Then I pressed send.

The next morning there was an email from her. As I wrote, it's been many years since that letter, but this is what I remember:

Dear Mr. Evans,
You have no idea how ashamed I am for writing such a hateful letter to you. I made a stupid mistake in buying the wrong book and, in my embarrassment, I blamed it on you. But then, far worse than that, I insulted you. Not just once but many times. I questioned your heart and ascribed the worst of motives to you. I demonized you.

But instead of responding with the anger I deserved, you reached out to me with kindness. You treated me with respect—me, a woman you will never meet and have no reason to care about. I believe you are exactly who you seem to be, Mr. Evans, a kind man I was afraid to believe could really exist. Please, Mr. Evans, do not write back. Please do not waste another moment

of your valuable time on someone as careless as me. I
do not deserve your forgiveness or to be treated with
such kindness. Please accept my sincerest apology.

I admit that my eyes welled up. Then I thanked God for
letting me be a better man than I might have been. I prayed
for this dear woman and her pain. I prayed that this "stranger"
would have peace in her life. How grateful I was that I had listened to my heart and not returned evil for evil.

When slights come into our lives—and they will—and
we're tempted to strike back, let's remember the words of a
wise teacher who once said, "Love your enemies, do good to
those who hate you, bless those who curse you . . ." Or, in the
words of the great statesman Abraham Lincoln, "Do I not destroy my enemies when I make them my friends?"

It's not easy to repay evil with good. But it's what love requires of us.

WHAT I LEARNED FROM
A FALSE DIAGNOSIS

I was writing my sixth novel, *The Carousel*, when, for reasons I don't remember, I decided to give one of my characters multiple sclerosis, a crippling disease of the central nervous system. Ironically, at that time, I hadn't been feeling very well, and, one afternoon, as I did research on the disease, I realized I had nearly all the symptoms of MS.

I was so disturbed by this discovery that I decided to get my mind off my worry by watching TV. As the television came on, the first words I heard were, "My feet and hands are numb. They feel like blocks. I keep dropping things . . ."

I couldn't believe it. They were the exact symptoms I was experiencing. In the next scene, the character was diagnosed with MS. (I was watching a movie about Annette Funicello.) It was such a bizarre coincidence that I thought it must be a sign. I made an appointment with my doctor.

That afternoon, I told my wife I had something to tell her. She looked at me with obvious anxiety.

"Did you have an affair?" she asked.

Her question threw me. "What? Of course not. Why would you ask that?"

"You look so . . . worried."

"I am. I think I have MS. I've made a doctor's appointment to have it checked out."

Honestly, I think she was a little relieved. She hugged me. "It's probably nothing," she said hopefully.

A week later I got in to see the doctor. He gave me a physical, and then, to my relief, said, "I don't know why you're having these symptoms, but I don't think it's MS. Still, we should probably do a CT scan just to put your mind at ease."

I left relieved but still cautious, and still not feeling well. I did a lot of thinking during that week. What if I did have the disease? How would my life change? I decided to make a list of things I wanted to do while I could still walk. One of the items on my list was to take my children to the Smithsonian Institution museums in Washington, DC—especially the National Air and Space Museum, which had wowed me as a child. I even went as far as to book the trip.

The morning we were to leave for Washington, I went with Keri to talk to the doctor and get the results of my CT scan. I've heard it said that if the jury doesn't look at you when they come back into the courtroom, you're going to hang. The doctor walked into the room without looking at me. He put my scans against the light box, then turned back and said, "It looks like you have MS."

My chest froze. He pointed to the scan with a pen. "See these marks? They're lesions on your brain." He slowly breathed out. "Sorry."

For a moment neither of us spoke. Then Keri, brushing back tears, said, "What now?"

"It's best that you see a specialist and work out your next steps. I can give you a referral if you like."

"I'd appreciate that," I said.

Keri cried on the way home. I didn't know what to say.

While in DC I visited with my friend the famed thriller writer David Baldacci. I gave him my news. He listened with understanding, then said, "My sister has MS. I sit on the board of the Virginia MS Society. There are a lot of new treatments they're working on. We're going to find a cure. It's just a matter of time."

I was grateful for his comforting words in a difficult time. When I got back home, I began seeking out people with MS. I wanted to learn firsthand what I should expect my life to be like. I found three people. One of them has since passed. They each told me, surprisingly, very much the same thing.

The first man I spoke with was deep in the throes of MS. He was extremely thin, and his body looked painfully racked with the disease. He was barely able to walk with a cane. He told me that prior to his diagnosis he had been a successful executive with a Fortune 500 company.

"I was gone all the time," he said. "All the time. I was focused only on my career. My family was just an obstacle to my career goals. I was a bad husband and an even worse father. Then came this." He looked down at his cane. "When I was diagnosed, I went through the usual stages of grief—denial, anger, depression, bargaining, and then, eventually, acceptance. It was only then, as I faced my new reality, that I mentally came home and found what I had been missing. What I had foolishly sacrificed." He looked tenderly at his wife, who had tears in her eyes. She squeezed his hand. "It was worth it," he said. "I might have lost her. I never would have really known my family. I wasn't happy before. I'm so grateful for this blessing."

Another thing I discovered was also surprising. As frightened as I was, there was also a powerful sense of relief. I realized that I too had been sprinting on the treadmill of success and I was spiritually, as well as physically, exhausted. I could finally stop running.

For the first time in my life, I gave myself permission to not only stop to smell the roses but maybe even plant a few rosebushes. I made a new life plan, along with a bucket list of everything I wanted to share and do with the people I loved while I still could. I worked less and spent more time with my wife and children. We took one of those family vacations we had talked about but never got around to.

Finally, almost six weeks later, I got in with the MS specialist. I still remember walking into his office and seeing those hateful CT scans of my brain hanging on the light box on his wall.

The doctor asked me a few questions and then said, "I'm not impressed."

"You're not impressed with what?" I asked.

"Your diagnosis. MS can be tricky to diagnose. Maybe you

have MS, but not according to these scans." He pointed out that in some rare cases, blood vessels in the brain mimic lesions. "I don't know why you have the symptoms you say you're having, but if you put a gun to my head I'd say you don't have it."

I went home relieved and very confused.

"Now what?" Keri asked.

I thought for a moment, then said, "Nothing changes. This was a gift."

After a few more months, my symptoms mysteriously disappeared. Maybe I have MS, maybe I don't. But it's been years since I've had any symptoms.

MS is a nasty and painful disease. Millions suffer from it. Every year, many die from its complications. In no way am I trying to minimize their suffering and loss. And yes, I'm very grateful I don't seem to have it. Still, I'm thankful for that misdiagnosis and what I learned from it.

DOUBLE JEOPARDY

> Each day I wake in the court of conscience to be
> judged guilty and unworthy. In this sorry realm I am
> the judge, prosecutor, and jury, and, without defense,
> I accept the verdict and the sentence, a lifetime of
> regret and guilt to be administered by myself.
> —*The Mistletoe Promise*

Have you ever punished yourself for a mistake over and over? Learning to forgive ourselves is difficult for many of us, but especially for the most caring among us—those with kind, sensitive hearts. (I'm pretty sure sociopaths don't have this problem.)

Not only do these good people condemn themselves harshly but, in a true act of injustice, they also try themselves over and over for the same offense. There's a name for this—*double jeopardy*—and it was considered an act of such injustice to America's founding fathers that they specifically added this line to the Fifth Amendment to the

Constitution: "Nor shall any person be subject for the same offense to be twice put in jeopardy of life or limb . . ."

The goal of the double jeopardy amendment is to avoid multiple prosecutions for the same crime. Yet that is precisely what many of us do to ourselves. We try ourselves repeatedly for the same offense, inflicting multiple punishments of self-hate, shame, and rejection. This is wholly unjust and wrong.

There is nothing wrong with feeling guilt for doing wrong. In fact, people who don't feel guilt scare me a little. But once we have acknowledged our mistakes and, if possible, made amends, the just and right thing is to let it go. Holding on to past wrongs is as foolish as a professional basketball player perseverating over a missed shot in a previous game. It not only distracts from the current game but also increases the chance of repeating the same mistake.

There is another reason to pursue self-forgiveness. Oftentimes we specifically attack others for the crimes we are unable to forgive in ourselves. The act of forgiving ourselves opens us up to the possibility of forgiving others.

So how do we forgive ourselves?

It begins with a decision to do so. But it usually takes more than that. Since humans are ritualistic by nature, here's an idea someone shared with me that helped: Take a piece of paper and write down your mistake in detail. Be very specific—when it took place, who was harmed, and how many times you've punished yourself for the error. (You'll probably have to estimate, as the number could be unknowable.) Then burn it in the backyard barbecue or firepit. Let it go. Be free.

The memory of your mistake may come again, as punishing yourself might have become a mental habit, but don't worry. When the thought pops back into your mind, this time you'll counter it with, "Nope, already processed that." Eventually your self-condemnation will completely vanish.

Remember, in considering past offenses, both yours and others, the key question to ask isn't whether anyone was wronged but, rather, what are you gaining by your lack of forgiveness? Victimhood is a cage, and you hold the key. Let yourself out.

TWO CLICHÉS SMART PEOPLE WON'T USE

"Avoid clichés" is one of the first things a writing instructor worth her pencils will teach. Clichés are signs not only of unoriginality but of lazy thinking in general—a truth that applies to speech as well as the printed word. But some clichés are worse than others. They are not just lacking in originality but, to my way of thinking, in intelligence as well. Here are two clichés that especially annoy me. Avoid them like the plague. (Yes, that's a joke.)

Dumb Cliché #1: "I'm not perfect."

What the proud bearer of this cliché fails to recognize is just how remarkably arrogant this statement is. Not perfect? Really? You? Imagine that. All this time everyone thought you were perfect. Sure, maybe you can't walk on water, but didn't you once feed a football stadium with three hot dogs and a tray of nachos?

What makes this cliché especially insidious is how often it's invoked by people who have just committed some heinous act. "Yeah, I killed him, Officer. I'm not perfect." Believe me, no one was expecting perfection from you, but a modicum of decency would have been nice.

The next time you catch yourself using this cliché, do yourself, and the world, a favor and cut out your tongue.

Dumb Cliché #2: "There are two sides to every story."

There are multiple variations of this stale chestnut; for example, "No matter how thin the pancake, it still has two sides," "Every coin has two sides," blah, blah, blah.

Right? Tell that to the four-year-old I saw in the hospital last year who had been raped and then beaten unconscious by her mother's boyfriend. I'm sure the boyfriend's side of the story warranted all our consideration.

Or maybe if someone had shared this cliché with the millions of people who were tortured and murdered by Hitler, Stalin, or Pol Pot, the victims might have felt much better about their deaths—because even despots have their sides of the story, right? Same pancake, same coin?

This lazy "two sides" cliché is nothing more than moral relativism at its worst. And, like a compass with no needle, it's useless.

I'm not saying there aren't reasons people do what they do. It's Psych 101. People always have reasons for their behavior no matter how depraved it might be. Rather, I'm stating the self-evident truth that there is evil in this world. And the way this cliché gives evil the same standing as charity, mercy, and civility is an evil in itself.

This also includes the sister cliche "There's good and bad in all of us"—another mindless cliché that's similar to comparing bottled water to sewage. Yes, they are both primarily H_2O, but one is clearly better to drink. But smart people already know that.

THE POWER OF GRATITUDE

M any years ago one of my daughters came to me laughing.

"I just saw the dumbest woman," she said. "Someone told her I was your daughter, and she went all crazy and weird."

I looked at my daughter for a moment, then asked, "What did she look like?"

My daughter looked at me quizzically. "What?"

"What did she look like?"

"I don't know. Just kind of normal."

"How tall was she?"

"Mom's size."

"What color hair?"

"Why are you asking me this?"

"What color?"

"I don't know, light brown."

"I know who she is," I said.

My daughter just stared at me. "You do?"

"Yes," I said, looking into my daughter's eyes. "She's the woman who bought those clothes you're wearing. She's also the woman who bought your school lunch last year and started your college fund. She's the one who paid for our last family vacation."

My daughter frowned. "I get it."

"I hope so," I said. "The next time you meet one of my readers, you thank them for the wonderful life they've given us. You tell them how grateful you are that your father gets to do something he loves for a living."

Sure, I was a bit dramatic, but I wanted to be clear with her about the importance of gratitude—as well as the danger of its absence. The lack of gratitude is a downward spiral that actually deters the blessings from which gratitude may be derived.

Gratitude is a rare *upward* spiral. When we are grateful for what we have, it brings new things to be grateful for. Studies show gratitude increases levels of well-being, happiness, energy, health, and empathy. Grateful people sleep better, cope better, and have better relationships, less depression, and less stress. Gratitude has even been medically proven to reduce headaches, stomach pain, coughing, and sore throats. Simply put, grateful people have better lives than those who aren't grateful.

So how does one become more grateful? Most people don't realize that gratitude is not just a serendipitous emotion but a skill. And, like all skills, it can be improved and cultivated.

It takes intent, discipline, and action to improve. It takes reminders. Start by writing at least one thank-you letter a day. Creating a personal gratitude routine is also a powerful way to develop this skill. On my Facebook page I started a weekly post called GratiTuesday, to remind myself and my readers to be grateful. If you're not feeling gratitude on a daily basis, you are depriving yourself of its power in your life.

FAILURE IS NOT AN OPTION

L ately I've been pondering why it is that when we set out to do something good we face so much adversity. Sometimes it even feels like we're being punished by the universe for trying to do the right thing.

A few weeks ago I attended a board meeting for the Christmas Box International—a charitable organization I founded several decades ago to help abused and neglected children. As our director read an impressive list of the year's accomplishments, my mind went back decades earlier to one of our first board meetings—a painful, agonizing one.

Back then, it seemed, nothing was going right. Community donations were a fraction of what we'd hoped for while our first shelter, which was still under construction, was a money pit—six months behind schedule and more than a half million dollars over budget. I had used up nearly all my savings building the shelter and now I couldn't even qualify for a loan to finish it. And we still hadn't helped a single child.

We had no shelter, no money, no community support, and abused children with no place to go. Surely there couldn't be a more worthy cause than helping abused children, I reasoned. So why did it seem that the universe was set against us?

As we were beginning that board meeting, my father, who sat on the board, asked to speak.

"Before we go any further," he said, "I'd like to make a motion. I'm sorry to say this, but this clearly isn't working. This shelter has nearly bankrupted my son. I make a motion that we close down the project."

His words were met with stunned silence. Then, to my surprise, our executive director spoke up. "I'd like to second the motion," he said. "The community just hasn't rallied around this cause like we hoped."

As I looked around the table, everyone seemed to concur. Finally, I asked, "Is that how you all feel?" Almost all the board members nodded in agreement. I sat quietly for a moment pondering the motion. Honestly, it would have been a relief to stop. At times the stress and discouragement of the project seemed more than I could take.

"Just a moment," I said, excusing myself. Walking out of the conference room I ducked into the only room in the office not occupied—a mechanical closet. There I knelt next to a water heater to pray. I asked God one question. *May I quit?*

There are likely times in most of our lives when we ask ourselves, "How did I get here?" This was one of those times. Except I knew how I had gotten there. I just wasn't sure where I was going.

The whole process of starting this charity began in the parking lot of a financial advisor's office. My wife and I had, a few weeks earlier, received a large advance from a publisher for my first book, *The Christmas Box*. Seeking help on handling such a large sum of money, I had set up an appointment with one of the myriad financial consultants who had descended upon us as soon as the local and national newspapers publicized our good fortune. As the advisor outlined how to build trusts to carefully pass money on to our children after they became drug addicts or alcoholics, ruined by fortune and fame, Keri and I were stunned. I had written my book to celebrate my children, not destroy them.

After the meeting we walked out to our minivan and sat in its open doorway to talk.

"Let's give the money back," Keri said.

"That's not going to happen," I said. Then I looked at her. "Money isn't inherently evil," I said. "It's just power. And like all power, good or bad is in how it's used. Why don't we teach our children how money should be used?"

"What are you thinking?"

"Let's start a charity."

She thought for a moment, then said, "Maybe we could help children. Children at risk."

That simple conversation set in motion hundreds of hours of meetings and opened doors at the highest levels of state government. Our first act was to sponsor a conference and ask a simple question: What is the most important thing we can do to help at-risk children?

The result of that conference was the concept of the Christmas Box House, a shelter to house abused and neglected children while smart decisions could be made about their future.

Utahns are known for their generosity, and I assumed, incorrectly, that the community would be quick to jump on board. But they didn't. Our first donations were checks for ten or twenty dollars, almost inconsequential when you're building a two-million-dollar facility. Keri and I ended up funding more than 95 percent of the charity, including the building and salaries. And it was quickly breaking us. We had already used up almost all our money, and now we were taking out loans to keep things going. It had long ago stopped being fun. Now it was threatening our financial existence.

So there I was, on my knees, six inches from a water heater, asking God if I could quit. The impression I received was unmistakable. *If you fail, no one else will succeed.*

I took a deep breath, got up off my knees, and walked back into the meeting. Looking around the table I said, "Thank you for your concern for my well-being, but I'm not quitting."

"You don't know what you don't know," our director said. "It's a sinking ship."

"Then I guess I'll be going down with it," I replied. "You're free to join me or not."

The room went silent. Then, after a minute or so, our director said, "All right. Let's get on with business."

The next week I printed up T-shirts for the board and staff with these words:

FAILURE IS NOT AN OPTION

For the next few months we continued to painfully limp along. Then one day I received a call from a friend of mine. A wealthy man whom she had told about the shelter wanted to know more. (He has asked to remain anonymous.) Several days later I gave him a tour of the unfinished facility. Afterward he asked me how things were going.

"Not as we'd hoped," I said. "It's just about bankrupted me."

He looked at me with surprise. "You put your own money into this?"

"Almost all of it," I answered.

He looked even more surprised. "I've never seen a celebrity use their own money," he said. "They usually just do fundraising events."

The next day I received a call from the man's assistant. "Mr. —— wanted me to call and let you know that he is wiring you a million dollars to help you finish your shelter."

Six months later, the shelter was completed and housing children. The first child to come through our doors was a baby taken from a meth house. I was blessed to be there and held that child. The shelter has been occupied every day since, for more than twenty-five years.

We went on to build a second shelter, and then a third. Since that time we've helped more than 145,000 children— enough to fill Madison Square Garden more than seven times. Many of those children are now adults raising their own children.

A few years ago I was signing books when I noticed a young blond teenager standing near the back of the line, staring at me. When she finally reached my table, she was nearly vibrating with excitement. She said, "Mr. Evans, my whole life I've wanted to meet you."

"You like my books?" I asked.

"Never read them," she responded.

Her reply made me grin. "Then why did you want to meet me?"

"I'm one of your Christmas Box House kids," she replied. She went on to explain that her biological parents were drug addicts and when the state took her and her brother away, no one wanted both of them. "We lived in your shelter until Mom and Dad adopted us. Our caseworker said that if it wasn't for you, I would have been raised without my brother." She put her arm around the teenage boy next to her. "I've always wanted to thank you for my brother."

That was a beautiful moment—and a sharp contrast to the first four years of frustration, panic attacks, and misery. I remember during those years feeling angry that everything seemed to go wrong. Many times I felt abandoned by God.

Since then I've come to believe there are two reasons our good deeds are met with opposition. The first is to allow us the opportunity to prove to ourselves the level of our commitment. It's been said that adversity introduces a man to himself. This is true. If all worthy endeavors were easy, there would be no greatness or nobility in the world. Just expediency and self-interest.

The second reason is more pragmatic. More times than not we do not succeed in spite of our challenges and obstacles but precisely because of them. It is the struggle itself that gives a thing life. Thoreau wrote, "All misfortune is but a stepping stone to fortune."

In my case, going through the challenges of building the shelter forced me to take a more active role in the organization's development and management. Without those challenges, our cause to help children would probably not have survived to today.

We all have causes—in our homes and in the world. As we overcome our challenges and obstacles, it is important to remember that oftentimes the rugged road we are forced to walk is the only path to our destination.

ON BEING KIND

Be kind. If you can't love your neighbors, be kind to them and you may see your kindness turn to love. We see it all too often, the self-adoring virtue signalers who loudly proclaim their great love for the disadvantaged masses but hate their next-door neighbors. Humanity is not the vast, unfathomable ocean we speak about in distant, general terms; it is the lone starfish that washes up on the beach.

Kindness is a symptom of love. Too many think of love as weakness. It's not. Love is not the fluff of greeting cards, nor the satin-embroidered Valentine's Day pillow. Love is the hard, rocky shore that holds fast against the ocean's turbulent waves. Love is the soldier who lays down his life for his friends in the trenches. Love is the mother who goes to bed hungry so her children will have breakfast. Love is the opposite of self-interest, the disciples of which flee at the hint of self-sacrifice and, like the ethereal seeds of a dandelion, scatter to the wind at the first small breeze to find the next real thing.

ROUTE 36 AND IMAGINATION

Running east-west along the northern quadrant of Missouri is a two-hundred-mile stretch of asphalt that's part of US Route 36. The expressway follows a route from a bygone era—the former tracks of the Hannibal and St. Joseph Railroad.

My daughter Jenna was my research assistant on a book series I was working on about a man who walked across the United States, and she talked me into taking the route as we drove from one end of the country to the other, from Seattle, Washington, to Key West, Florida.

After crossing the length of South Dakota (stopping at the famous Wall Drug and the Corn Palace), we took Interstate 29 south from Sioux Falls through Omaha, and then, instead of continuing south to Kansas City, we turned our course east at St. Joseph.

St. Joseph, the beginning of Route 36, is a beautiful city with a historic past. At one point it was considered the end

of civilization as the last train stop before settlers moved their
baggage from train cars to covered wagons and headed west. It
was also the home and death place of Jesse James (you can still
see the hole from the bullet that passed through his head in
the living room wall of his house) and the origin of the short-
lived but iconic Pony Express.

I don't suppose many people go out of their way to drive
Route 36. The landscape is as dull as one of my editing pencils.
In fact, it was among the more unremarkable stretches we'd
encountered as we crossed the country. *Not much to see*, I initially
thought. But I was wrong. It's not the landscape but the history
that was worth the drive. The people who have emerged from
this nondescript scenery have changed the world.

After Jenna and I had traveled maybe an hour east on 36
from St. Joseph, I said to her, "Maybe we should have taken
Twenty-Nine down to Kansas City."

"Hang in there," she said. "There are things to be seen."

Before long we came to a sign that read:

Hamilton, Missouri
Boyhood home of J.C. Penney

James Cash Penney (his parents were clearly having fun
with that name) was born in Hamilton, Missouri. At its peak,
the Penney chain had more than two thousand stores. Walmart
founder Sam Walton got his start at one of those stores. Penney changed the way the retail world operated. And he came
from a little nowhere town.

"I guess you have to come from somewhere," I said to Jenna.

That *somewhere* I was referring to was just beginning. Not too much farther down the asphalt we came to a sign that read:

Laclede, Missouri
Boyhood home of Gen. John J. Pershing

We took the exit to see the general's home and monument. At one time, Pershing commanded more than three million soldiers and was conferred the rank of General of the Armies of the United States, making him the highest-ranking US military officer in history. In fact, President Gerald Ford posthumously raised George Washington's rank so that he would not be outranked by Pershing.

He also won the Pulitzer Prize in history for his two-volume memoir, *My Experiences in the World War*. The man had a tank and a missile named after him.

An hour later we continued our drive to a town called Chillicothe, whose city sign bragged:

Chillicothe
Home of Sliced Bread

I suspect people have been slicing bread for as long as there have been knives and bread, but it was Otto Rohwedder, a Chillicothe resident, who invented the bread slicer and made it not only the standard in bread preparation but a cliché as well.

The next exit of interest was Marceline—the boyhood home of Walt Disney. To Disney, it represented his halcyon days—his childhood era of joy and wonderment. Disney claimed that he patterned Disneyland's Main Street, USA, after his fond memories of this small town, which, after we drove through, showed that he really did have a powerful imagination. Or, maybe he just, like many of us, carried idealized childhood memories.

Our last stop on 36 was Hannibal, Missouri, legendary home of Samuel Langhorne Clemens, better known as Mark Twain, the man William Faulkner called the father of American literature.

"I was wrong about this road," I conceded. "This region of America changed the world. It makes me wonder what was in the water."

Of course it's not what was in the water. It was what was in these people's heads. The one thing these game changers all had in common was the ability to see beyond their staid rural reality and create a world that didn't exist around them. What they had was *imagination*.

Einstein claimed that imagination was more important than knowledge. Knowledge is finite. Imagination isn't. He was right, of course. If I could put a sign on every child's bedroom wall, it would say the following:

The success of your life is more determined by imagination than by circumstance

Imagination is the soil in which your future is planted. It is the power to see past the four walls around us, past borders, cultural and physical, even cosmic. It was the way these innovators saw past the dull landscape of Route 36. Perhaps the very dull nature of the terrain was why it was such fertile ground for innovation.

I once asked a successful friend of mine how she got to where she was in the world. She came from a tiny town with an abusive father who spent most of his life preparing for World War III. They lived on top of a mountain because her father believed he could blow up the road when the Russians invaded.

My friend told me that she spent her life imagining a world beyond her home, one far away from the small town and her father's paranoia. Her answer to my question was worth noting. "I just waited for reality to catch up with my imagination."

We can all learn from this. We can imagine ourselves into something better—a world of love and peace. We can imagine ourselves being the instruments to carry this out. We can imagine being good in the face of the world's darkness.

Lewis Carroll wrote, "Imagination is the only weapon in the war against reality."

Imagination is the greatest power we have to make a new world. Without imagination, as the renowned scientist Carl Sagan once said, "we go nowhere."

CHASING PRADA

Italy, of course, is known for its fashion, spawning globally recognized brands like Armani, Gucci, Versace, and Valentino. One of those famous brands is Prada, which had an outlet in the town of Montevarchi, about forty minutes from where my family was living at the time in Florence.

One summer my agent, Laurie, came to visit us for a week. She had done her pre-travel research, and one of the items on her Italy checklist was to stop at the Prada outlet. So, the day before her departure, Laurie, Keri, and I climbed into our Volvo station wagon and drove off to the outlet. Forty-five minutes later I turned off the autostrada for Montevarchi. As I approached the city's tollbooth, I asked Laurie which way I should turn after we passed through the gate.

"I actually didn't get that far," she said. "I thought we'd probably just see it when we got here. The town's bigger than I thought it would be."

Much bigger. Montevarchi has been around for nearly

a thousand years and covers almost twenty-two square miles. This was a few years before we all had GPS on our phones, so I pulled off to the side of the road to make a plan. Just then a delivery truck imprinted with the word *Prada* came through the gate we'd just passed through. Laurie shouted, "It's a Prada truck! Follow that truck."

I turned out into traffic behind it. The truck followed a circuitous route, through roundabouts, small streets, and neighborhoods. At times it almost felt like the driver was going in circles. Then, after nearly fifteen minutes, I suspected he knew I was following him and was trying to lose me, especially since he had waited at one light until it was just about to turn red before darting through the intersection. I ran the light after him. After nearly half an hour of this cat and mouse, I said, "I don't think he's going to the outlet."

"Just keep following him," Laurie said.

"I have to follow him now," I said. "I'm lost."

After another fifteen minutes he turned down a small side road and then jumped out of his truck, gesturing wildly. *"Che cosa!?"* (What!?)

I got out of the car and pointed to the Prada sign on his truck.

He nodded. *"Ma certo,"* he said. *"Un momento."* (Of course. One moment.)

He carried a package into a house, and when he came back he said, *"Segue mi."* (Follow me.)

We followed his truck to the Prada outlet, waving to him as we pulled into the parking lot. I let the women off at the door, then pulled out to park. As I got out of the car, the women were walking back toward me. The store had closed just five minutes earlier.

LIVING GRATITUDE

I've come to believe that few things in life will bring as quick a change in our world as the active pursuit of gratitude. I've also concluded that few virtues have as much power to alter the very foundation of who we are and where we're going.

In my own observation, I've learned a few things about the powerful virtue of gratitude.

First, gratitude is the key component of happiness. It is both the gateway and the destination. We do not feel grateful because we are *happy*, we feel happy because we are *grateful*. It may be impossible to separate the two. Conversely, those who choose lives of ingratitude are never happy.

Second, gratitude enhances our ability to receive and draw even more to be grateful for. This is simple to illustrate. Let's say neighbors bring you a plate of cookies. You accept the offering, then send them on their way without so much as a thank you. I guarantee you will never enjoy their cookies again. But, if you show demonstrative, sincere gratitude, you will likely be a regular recipient of their cookies for many years to come.

I've seen this principle demonstrated in more substantial ways than cookies. As chairman of a charitable foundation, I would not infrequently hear from new donors that they switched their donations to us because the charity they had donated many thousands of dollars to never bothered to thank them.

Another example. A friend once told me that his business was doing well so he decided to give his employees a generous Christmas bonus—a month's salary.

He said the first year he did this his employees were grateful and happy. But that changed. The second year, his employees expected the bonus, and only a few of them even bothered to thank him. By the third year, full entitlement had set in, and not one employee thanked him at all. Not even in passing. In fact, he told me, one of them even complained. A new employee had started working for him just a few weeks before Christmas and thought she "deserved" a full month's salary bonus like everyone else.

That's when he started giving out Christmas hams instead.

I don't blame him at all. Ingratitude deserves the wages it earns. Truly, there are none so impoverished as those who will not acknowledge the abundance of their lives.

UNEXPECTED
TEACHERS

LESSONS FROM THE VINEYARD

For more than a year, my wife and I lived just outside Florence, Italy, in the Chianti region where the famous Chianti wines are made. Every day I would look out our bedroom window and see the beautiful rolling hills ripe with blushing Sangiovese grapes and think, *Sembra una cartolina*, it looks just like a postcard.

One day I was out walking along a trail next to a vineyard when I came upon a farmer standing among his vines. Eager to practice my Italian, I said to the man, "This is a beautiful vineyard you have."

"*Tante grazie*," he replied.

"You must have very good soil to grow grapes that make famous wines."

The man looked at me and said, "No, signore. You cannot grow good grapes in good soil."

I thought his answer curious, so when I got back home I looked up grape farming on the internet. The farmer was right, of course. I learned that poor soil yields higher-quality grapes than good soil because the vines have to work harder, branching off more roots to gather nutrients. Not only does this increase the amount of nutrients that ultimately get to the grape but it also regulates how much water the plant gets—resulting in a grape with character.

This is an apt metaphor for us humans as well. Sometimes, difficulties rise before us like mountains. But mountains can raise us or bury us depending on which side we choose to stand. Both history and life teach us that, more times than not, we succeed not in spite of our challenges and difficulties but because of them.

Even a grape knows that.

WHAT I LEARNED FROM A PERUVIAN STREET BOY

Around the turn of the century, my wife and I helped build several orphanages in Peru. The first of those was called *Colibri*, the Hummingbird. On one visit, I had an interesting experience. As I entered the gate through an adobe wall, a small, wild-haired boy ran up to greet me. His face was as dirty as his clothes, and his sandals were made from car tires. What caught my attention most, though, was not the child's poverty but his smile—a grin that filled his face. The reason for his excitement, I learned, was that a local farmer had generously donated a cow to the orphanage and the boy had been given the important job of getting up early each morning to milk it.

He was clearly excited to have been given such a meaningful responsibility and he asked me if I would like to see how he separated the cream from the milk.

I thought about what a contrast there was between this wonderful little boy and the young American girl in a video

I had recently seen who threw a tantrum when her parents gave her the wrong color car for Christmas.

Before leaving the orphanage, we drove to a local store to purchase some groceries for the orphanage. That same little boy came to help us carry them. Almost as an afterthought, I bought him a candy bar. I suppose I had expected him to wolf it down like Charlie with a Wonka Bar. Instead, he just held it. I asked my native translator if the boy didn't like the type of candy bar I'd purchased. The man laughed at my question. "That is like asking if he did not like gold," he said.

"But he's not eating it."

"No, señor, he would never eat it by himself. He will take it back to his brothers at the orphanage and they will cut it into thirteen pieces so each boy can have a share of his good fortune."

I immediately purchased another dozen candy bars. *What a remarkable lesson*, I thought. *For me. For all of us. We should all be so quick to share our good fortune.*

A STRANGER ON A FLIGHT

I t had been one of those dreadful days of traveling. I had been flying from city to city on a book tour for more than two weeks and, as usual, the airports were slammed for the holidays. I had taken a crowded flight out of Cincinnati, only to find that my connecting flight to St. Louis had been delayed nearly four hours.

As I sat there, tired and bored, listening to the grumblings of disgruntled passengers, I noticed a young mother sitting on the ground next to the airline counter. She seemed oblivious to her young daughter running wildly around the area, further annoying many of the already stressed passengers.

After what seemed an eternity, our flight arrived and I had just taken my seat in first class when the young mother walked past me carrying her child. As she passed, I noticed her makeup was smeared and her eyes were red and puffy.

After everyone had boarded and the flight attendants were making last-minute preparations for takeoff, the young man seated across the aisle from me suddenly bolted from his seat and ran to the back of the plane. I assumed he was running to the bathroom. A flight attendant shouted at the man to return to his seat, and then, when he didn't, chased after him.

A moment later the flight attendant returned not with the young man but with the distraught young mother, who sat in the seat the man had vacated. The young man had given this woman his first-class seat. The woman was still crying and struggling with her daughter, so, after takeoff, I handed my iPad to the little girl to play with, then asked the woman how I could help. After gaining her composure, she said to me, "I'm sorry I'm such a mess. My husband died last night. My little girl doesn't understand. She keeps asking for her daddy."

I don't think it was a coincidence that she ended up sitting next to me. Having spoken to grief groups for many years, I was experienced in talking with the bereaved. I spent the next few hours consoling the woman.

At the end of the flight, the woman leaned over and hugged me and thanked me for being there. All I could think was that the real Good Samaritan had been the young man who gave up his seat. So, after disembarking, I waited for the young man, stopping him as he stepped out of the Jetway. I asked him if he knew that the woman he'd given his seat to had just lost her husband.

"No," he said softly. "She just looked like she needed some kindness."

Perhaps it was a small gesture, but it was a beautiful one nonetheless. In the midst of chaos and frayed tempers, this young man had reached out beyond himself to help a stranger in need. It's inspiring to know that that kind of goodness is still alive in this world.

WHAT A HOMELESS MAN TAUGHT ME ABOUT SUCCESS

Some years ago I was invited to be the keynote speaker at a writers' conference in San Francisco. My wife, Keri, had always wanted to see the city, so we turned the event into a short vacation. At the top of my wife's bucket list was to ride one of the city's famous cable cars.

After my presentation, Keri and I took a cab to the main trolley station only to find that a multitude of others had the same idea and there was a line more than three blocks long.

I asked a woman near the front of the line how long she had been waiting. "Hours," she said gruffly. I didn't want to wait that long, but Keri had her heart set on the experience and, not wanting to disappoint her, I joined her at the back of the line. What made the wait even more frustrating was that it appeared that the trolley cars were leaving the station just half-full, doubling our wait time.

Then Keri dropped her cell phone. The thing practically exploded on the sidewalk, with pieces flying everywhere. Before either of us could gather up the pieces a homeless man, who had been working the line asking for money, picked up a piece of Keri's phone and handed it to me.

"Here you go," he said. I was expecting him to ask for money but instead he asked, "You waiting for the trolley?"

"Yes."

"This line is more than an hour," he said.

"That's what I heard."

He scratched his beard. "For a dollar I'll tell you a secret to getting on the car in five minutes."

It was an intriguing proposition. Frankly, I would have given him the money anyway, but now I was curious to hear what he had to say.

"All right." I handed him a dollar.

"Thank you," he said, shoving the bill in his pocket. "Here's the secret. Have you noticed that the trolley cars leave the station only half-full?"

I nodded and said yes.

"They do that because there are stops all the way up the road. If the cars were already full they couldn't pick anyone up, right? The stops are marked by a white *X* painted in the road." He pointed directly across the street from where we were standing. "See that *X* right there? That's the first stop."

"Right in front of us?" I said.

"Yes, sir. I wouldn't lie to you," he said, then added, "Was that good enough for another dollar?"

"Absolutely." I handed him another bill, and then Keri and I walked across the street and stood in front of the X. Within a few minutes a trolley car stopped right in front of us. X marked the spot.

As we stepped onto the trolley, a woman already sitting inside just gaped at us. "I waited almost two hours," she said dolefully.

In nearly every human endeavor there are queues or obstacles between what we want and where we are. We've come to expect them. We even look for them. But many of them aren't necessary. I've met way too many people who have trained themselves to find the obstacles that hinder their dreams. Some people, afraid to lose their place in line, wait their whole lives when they could just cross the street.

Keri is a good example of someone crossing the street to fulfill their dream. After living in Florence, Italy, for nearly two years, she decided she wanted to start a travel company taking people on tours of the country. She made plans to go back to college to study Italian and art history. She figured it would take her about four years to start her tour company.

"Too long," I said. "You'll learn more preparing and guiding your first tour than you would in four years of college. Just do it."

She decided to take my advice and reached out to a local travel agency to partner with her. Only six months later, she took her first group to Italy, which, by all accounts, was a resounding success. Since then she's taken more than a thousand people to the old country and her tours are wildly popular. By throwing herself in the ring, she's not only learned more about the country's language and history, she's learned how to run a successful business.

The great author and speaker Og Mandino wrote: "In truth, experience teaches thoroughly, yet her course of instruction devours men's years so the value of her lessons diminishes with the time necessary to acquire her special wisdom. The end finds it wasted on dead men."

I've found that postponing our dreams is the surest way to kill them. And, as the homeless man pointed out to us, our dreams are oftentimes a lot closer and more accessible than we think. Sometimes the secret is to focus on the desire instead of the obstacle and find the painted Xs that are right in front of us.

THE TONGAN TEENAGER
WHO CLEANED MY OFFICE

Peculiarly, my home state of Utah has a statistically high number of Pacific Islanders: Samoans, Fijians, and especially Tongans. Tonga is an archipelago in the South Pacific, somewhere between Fiji, Samoa, and New Zealand.

A look at the Utah football rosters reveals names like Kaufusi and Fualalo and Tuipulotu. (It's always amusing listening to the announcers trying to get the names right.) There's professional golfer Tony Finau. One of every four Tongans in the US lives in Utah.

When I was just starting my career in advertising, one of these young men from the islands cleaned the downtown office building where I ran my small agency and animation studio. He went to West High School, which, as it sounds, is on the west side. West is the oldest public high school in Utah and had the reputation of being a tough inner-city school.

I was working late one night when this young man came in to empty my trash cans. I had had the same job when I was a few years younger than him.

I stopped what I was doing and turned to him. "You're new here."

"Yeah. Just started."

"What's your name?"

"Koloa."

"Does that mean something?"

"It means wealthy man."

"Are you a wealthy man?"

He laughed. "I'm emptying garbages," he said.

"Are you Tongan?"

"Yes."

"I'm Rick," I said. "It doesn't mean anything." I lifted a box from my desk. "Want a doughnut?"

"Sure." He took one. As he ate it he looked around my office and studio. "What do you do here?"

"We do clay animation."

"What's that?"

"Ever heard of the California Raisins?"

He smiled. "You did that?"

"No. But I do that kind of animation."

"Cool," he said. "Are you famous?"

"No. Just barely making a living."

Koloa and I became friends. Every night when he came by to empty my garbage he'd stop to talk. He wasn't large like most of the Tongans I'd met, but he was funny and strong and wiry and, apparently, good at football because, as a sophomore, he played varsity running back at West High School.

He usually wanted to talk about what I was working on, but I'd always ask him about his life as well. One day he said, "Living in America is a lot different from living in Tonga."

"In what way?"

"The laws. We're usually bigger than Americans. We can beat up the teachers and they can't do anything about it. In Tonga, the teachers would beat us up, but here they can't do anything."

"That's messed up," I said.

"Yeah. All around."

One day he came in so upset he almost didn't speak to me.

"What's wrong?" I asked.

"They're changing our school boundaries. I have to go to East High."

"East High is a good school."

"It's a bunch of rich white kids."

"You'll be all right," I said. "Give it a chance."

A few weeks later he came in happy. He was singing.

"You're in a good mood," I said.

"I went to a rich-white-people party last night."

"How did that go?"

"The house was really big. They had a swimming pool inside the house."

"How was the party?"

"It was fun. We started throwing everyone in the pool. And they had like really good food. A ton of it. And the people were cool. I got invited to another party next week."

"You're popular," I said.

"I think I am."

"I told you you would be all right."

A few months later I was working late to meet a deadline and I walked out of my building at two in the morning.

Just as the door locked behind me I realized I wasn't alone. There were at least a dozen other people around me, mostly huge young men. It was a gang of Pacific Islanders. Several of these mountains of flesh were leaning against my car smoking. A young man who looked like he could be a lineman for any NFL team walked up to me, his face set in a fierce, menacing expression. *This isn't going to end well*, I thought. When he was a few feet from me, I heard a voice say, "Hey, cool it, man. He's my friend."

I looked over. Koloa was leaning against the building.

The lineman stopped in front of me. I was amazed at how quickly his expression relaxed. "Sorry, brother. Didn't know," he said, raising a massive hand in friendship. We shook hands.

"It's all right," I said, happy to still be vertical.

A couple of nights later, Koloa brought several of the gang members to show them what I did. I especially remember this one massive kid with thick keloid knife scars all over his body.

We were preparing to shoot a commercial for a local television station and had created a large brick building made of clay, each brick individually made. He was in wonderment over it all and looked as excited as a boy at Disneyland.

"You made all this?" he asked.

"I have sculptors make them. I'm not as talented as they are."

"So cool," he said. "Is this going to be on TV?"

"Eventually."

"Cool, man. Are you famous?"

"No. Just making a living."

As they were leaving my studio, I stopped Koloa. "Hey, about the other night. Thanks for having my back."

He shrugged. "Of course. We're friends."

"Friends? Because I gave you a doughnut?"

"No, because you're the only one in this building who's ever talked to me."

It was a small thing that might have saved my life.

MARRIAGE, FAMILY, AND OTHER BLESSINGS

A TURKEY FEATHER

My ranch in southern Utah is graced with flocks of wild turkeys. During one of our visits, my daughter Abigail, four years old at the time, handed me a picture she'd just colored—a crayon drawing of a turkey.

"I drew that for the turkeys," she said.

I admired her art. "Good job, buddy."

"Thank you, Dad," she said. "If you see a turkey, will you ask him if he'll trade a feather for it?"

I smiled. "Of course."

Later that afternoon, I was sitting on the front deck of the ranch house reading when a flock of turkeys strutted by. Remembering Abigail's desire for a feather, I got up and chased after them. They quickly left me in the dust, but in their frenzied escape, one of them also left a large feather. I picked it up and took it to Abigail.

"There you are, honey," I said.

She smiled. "Thank you, Dad."

I started to walk away when she said, "Dad?"

I turned back. "Yes?"

"Did he like my picture?"

WHAT MY SEVEN-YEAR-OLD DAUGHTER TAUGHT ME ABOUT LOVE

The task of defining love is one that philosophers, theologians, and psychologists have wrestled with for millennia. Personally, I found a pretty good definition in Italy.

One Sunday, while my family was living in Florence, a young Italian woman who had befriended us walked up to me, kissed me on both cheeks, then said, "Richard, *ti voglio bene*."

I had only started learning Italian and didn't understand her. "I'm sorry, what did you say?"

"*Ti voglio bene*," she repeated more slowly.

"I don't know what that means," I replied.

She rolled her eyes, then exclaimed in English, "I love you!"

I said to my wife, Keri, who speaks Italian, "Doesn't *ti amo* mean 'I love you'?"

Keri replied, *"Ti amo* is romantic love. *Ti voglio bene* literally means 'I want good for you.'"

What a beautiful definition of love.

A few weeks later I saw this kind of love demonstrated by my seven-year-old daughter, Abigail, at a public swimming pool.

Although Abigail was a pretty good swimmer, she was still afraid of deep water, so she stayed at the shallow end where her feet could touch the bottom. At the opposite end of the pool, her three-year-old brother Michael, who couldn't swim, was floating with his water wings.

I was sitting on a lounge chair at the side of the pool, reading a book, when I suddenly heard Abi shouting. I looked up to see her in the deep end of the pool, holding on to Michael's arm, struggling to keep her head above water.

"Abi!" I shouted. "Let go of him!"

She continued struggling, splashing in the water.

"Abi!" I shouted again. "You're going to drown both of you! Let go of him right now!"

Then the lifeguard did what I should have done: He dove into the pool and pulled them out of the water. Only after they were on dry ground did I learn what had happened. Abigail was at the other end of the pool when Michael jumped into the deep end, his arms above his head. One of his water wings had fallen completely off and the other had slid down to his elbow, leaving him underwater. Abigail was the only one who had seen what he'd done and, in spite of her tremendous fear of deep water, had jumped in to save her brother.

I can't think of a better example of true love—of *ti voglio bene*. Unlike "romantic" love, this healthy type of love is not as much to desire a person as it is to desire their well-being, their mental and spiritual growth.

Unfortunately, most vehicles of pop culture extol a version of love that psychologists call limerence, a psychological state of deep infatuation that, though exhilarating, doesn't last. Real love is not the briefly blooming flower but the thorny stem—the flower's protection and source of all nourishment and life. The love my daughter showed that day was something much more than is found in thousands of romance novels—something much more real.

I try to remember this every day—to look at others and say to myself, *Ti voglio bene*. I've found that it fosters peace not only in my relationships but inside my heart and mind as well. Try it. Think how much better this world would be if everyone did.

LITTLE GIRLS

No little girl can stop her world to wait for me.
—"How You've Grown," 10,000 Maniacs

A reporter once asked me why I had chosen a line from a 10,000 Maniacs song to use as an epigraph to my book *The Christmas Box*. As fitting as the words are to the book, I had an even more personal reason for its inclusion.

One night I was playing with my daughters Jenna and Allyson when "How You've Grown" came on the stereo. My daughters spontaneously began to dance, flinging themselves about in rapturous motion. I was lost in the joy of that moment. As I listened to the words, about the fleeting nature of childhood, I began to feel a little sentimental.

Allyson, who was only four at the time, suddenly asked, "Dad, what's wrong? There's water in your eyes."

I assured her that nothing was wrong, but she didn't

believe me. She came over and sat in my lap. There was, after all, *water in my eyes*. I told her that listening to the song made me think about them growing up.

"Don't you want us to grow up?" she asked.

"That's a hard question," I said. I told her I wanted her to grow up and have all the experiences life held for her. But I never wanted her to go away. And I never wanted this moment to end.

She thought about it for a moment, and then, with the music still playing in the background, she said, "Dad, then let's dance."

She got it right, I thought. *Dance*. Dance for the joy and brevity of childhood. Dance for all children, including that child who is entombed deep inside each of us beneath the responsibility and cynicism of adulthood. Embrace the moment before it forever escapes our grasp. For the only promise of childhood, any childhood, is that it will someday end.

As I write in one of my books, "Sunsets, like childhood, are viewed with wonder not just because they are beautiful but because they are fleeting."

My girls no longer live with me. Jenna is a writer like me. Allyson just got her doctorate as a nurse anesthetist. They have all left the nest, just as I knew they someday would. But the memories remain, growing sweeter with time. 10,000 Maniacs was right. No little girl can stop the world to wait for me.

MY DAUGHTER, BONO, AND GRATITUDE

"**I**'m the luckiest girl in the world," my daughter Jenna once told me. She meant it. I don't think it's so much that Jenna *has* a great life—she would be the first to tell you that she does—but that she *appreciates* her life. In my experience, people are not grateful because they're happy; rather, they're happy because they're grateful.

In my daughter's case, she's always been quick to see the positive in her experiences and express gratitude. I believe it's precisely this attitude that attracts more good. For instance, back when Jenna was a teenager, she confided in me that one of her bucket-list items was to see Bono—the lead singer and songwriter of the legendary Irish rock group U2—in concert.

Jenna had been a longtime Bono fan, even, as a young woman, going so far as to hunt down his boyhood home in Dublin's tough Northside suburb of Finglas. (Fortunately, a concerned Irishman picked her up, warning her that it wasn't the kind of place that a "young American lady should be a wanderin' about.")

So when Jenna found out that U2 was coming to play our hometown of Salt Lake City, she could hardly contain herself. "I can't wait," she told me. "I just hope I can get tickets before they sell out."

She didn't. The concert sold out in minutes. She was disappointed, but in typical fashion she shrugged it off. "I guess it just wasn't meant to be," she said.

A few months later, still several weeks before the concert, I was speaking at a company's Christmas party when the owners began giving away prizes to their employees. The company had had an especially prosperous year and I watched in amazement as they gave away hundreds of gifts: everything from iPods to snowmobiles. One of the prizes was a U2 package featuring a book on U2, a U2 purse, and two tickets to the band's upcoming concert. Noticing that the winner didn't seem especially excited about what he'd won, I asked him if he would be willing to sell his tickets.

"Sure," he said. "I have no idea who these guys are."

I purchased the tickets and the next day informed Jenna that I had a surprise for her. As I got ready to give her what I thought would be the surprise of a lifetime, I made an awful discovery. The tickets I'd bought had been purchased separately, so the seats weren't even close to each other, which meant she would essentially be going to the concert alone. Suddenly my surprise didn't seem so great.

When I showed Jenna the tickets, she was ecstatic, throwing her arms around me. "You're so good to me."

"It's not as great as it sounds," I replied. "The tickets aren't together. I'm sorry."

Jenna laughed. "You bought me tickets to U2 and you're apologizing? Are you kidding? You're the best dad ever! Besides, things will work out."

Honestly, how could you not love giving to someone so grateful?

Jenna invited her younger sister Allyson to go to the concert with her. The night of the concert my daughters again thanked me for the tickets and left for the show. A few hours later, I received a call from Jenna's phone. I answered to blaring music.

"Jenna?"

"Dad," she shouted. "You'll never believe where I am. I'm literally three feet from Bono. I just got his sweat on me."

"Bono's sweating on you?"

"I'll tell you about it later," she said. "Got to go. Thank you, thank you, thank you."

Later that night, Jenna told me what had happened. As my daughters were entering the concert, a gigantic, tattoo-covered security guard looked the girls over, then said in a thick Irish brogue, "Just a moment, please. I need to check your tickets."

Jenna quizzically handed the man her ticket. He ran it through a machine and then shook his head. "I'm sorry. This ticket's no good."

Jenna's heart froze. "What? My dad bought them."

"I'm sorry, but it's no good." He turned to my other daughter. "Let me see yours." Allyson anxiously surrendered her ticket to the man. He frowned. "Just as I thought. This one's no good either. I'm afraid you're going to need these." He handed my daughters DayGlo orange wristbands. Jenna looked at the guard. "What are these?"

"Like I said, your tickets weren't any good. So I'm putting you on the stage with the band."

"Are you serious?"

He smiled. "Say hi to Bono for me."

Jenna squealed. "May I hug you?"

The giant guard smiled. "Sure. I'll take that."

Life has taught me that there are none so poor as those who will not acknowledge the blessings in their lives. But those who remember to be thankful for their blessings seem to attract a whole lot more to be thankful for.

THE ONLY WAY TO FLY

After spending a lovely week in Virginia at my author friend David Baldacci's lake house, our family headed back home to Salt Lake City, flying out of Ronald Reagan Washington National Airport in Arlington. When we arrived at the gate, we were informed that our flight had been delayed four hours. Delayed flights are never fun, but at the time, we had a large, young family—two two-year-olds, a six-year-old, and two teenagers—and the children, after being in the car for three hours, were already a bit wild.

As I sat there in the crowded terminal watching the little ones rage like an unchecked forest fire, I looked at our tickets to see what section of the plane our tribe would be blessing. That's when I realized that the airline had, inexplicably, scattered our seats throughout the plane. Not one of us was sitting next to any of the others.

I walked up to the gate agent, who was clearly not having his best day.

"There's been a mistake," I said, laying out our boarding passes. "None of our seats are together."

"You should have booked them together," he said.

"We did."

"If you did, they would be together, wouldn't they?"

Employee of the month, I thought. "Look," I said, doing my best to remain civil. "The tickets were all booked at the same time. We were all together coming out here. I had no reason to believe your airline would scatter them going back."

"Well, there's nothing I can do about that now," he replied. "The flight's oversold."

"But two of our children are two years old," I said. "Are they supposed to sit alone?"

"Sorry," he said. (Clearly he was not.) "There's nothing I can do."

"I'd like to speak with a manager," I said.

"We're all a little busy right now," he said curtly. "I'll page you when she can talk."

I went back and told Keri about the situation.

"You've got to be kidding," she said. "They can't do that."

"Well, they did. And they're not too concerned about it."

After an hour we still hadn't heard anything, so I walked back up to the gate agent. Before I opened my mouth he said, "I told you we'll get to it when we can."

I walked back to my seat. Keri and I were exhausted. As I went back to herding the kids, it occurred to me that I had been going about this all wrong. I walked back up to the gate agent.

His eyes flashed when he saw me. "I told you . . ."

"No," I said, holding my hand up to stop him. "No worries. I just wanted to tell you everything's fine. Thanks for your help."

He looked at me blankly. "What?"

"We're okay. You don't have to change our seats. Thanks."

He looked at me suspiciously. "Why don't you care anymore?"

I looked over at my kids, one of whom was chewing on a chair. "These kids have been in a car or the airport for six hours and they're out of control. We're perfectly happy letting someone else watch our kids for the next four hours. Thank you for the free babysitting." I slapped the counter. "So, we're good." I turned and walked away.

Five minutes later I was paged to the ticket desk. Without a word, the agent handed me seven tickets all next to each other. I should have just kept my mouth shut.

FINDING MY DAUGHTER

Shakespeare wrote that "there's a divinity that shapes our ends." I believe that. To me, this story is a prime example of that kind of divine intervention. It is about how our daughter McKenna came to us from China.

It was an ordinary summer afternoon. I was driving home from work when I suddenly felt a prompting to turn on the radio. I turned the radio on to catch the last part of an NPR program about the growing number of abandoned girls in China. I listened for just a few minutes when I felt another prompting, this one even stronger than the first.

One of those children is yours, it said. *Go get her.*

Adoption was not something Keri or I were thinking about or had ever discussed. Still, I picked up my cell phone.

"I think we're supposed to adopt a Chinese girl," I said to Keri, feeling a little crazy as the words came out of my mouth. To my surprise, she said okay, as casually as if I'd just asked if we could have chicken for dinner. This was a bit out of character for my wife. Keri tends to take her time before making most decisions, especially the big ones. For instance, Keri had burned through three very annoyed real estate agents before deciding on a home to buy. And adding a child to a family is one of the biggest decisions anyone can make.

That night, at dinner, I said to her, "Were you serious about adopting a baby from China?"

She nodded. "Yes."

Suddenly Jenna, our nine-year-old, said, "Mom, my dream!"

Keri's expression changed to surprise. "Oh my. Yesterday Jenna told me she dreamt that we adopted a Chinese baby."

The next morning, my agent called from New York. "I had the strangest dream last night," she started. "I dreamt that I went with your family to Disney World. But every time I turned around there was a little Chinese girl following us."

My heart skipped a beat. I told her about the day before.

"What are you going to do?" she asked.

"I don't know. But it feels like it's pursuing us, so I guess we'll find out."

That weekend I went to a family reunion where I ran into a cousin, a lawyer, I hadn't seen for a few years. "How's your practice going?" I asked.

"Good," he said. "But lately I've been doing something a little different. I've been specializing in foreign adoptions."

I told him about what had happened to us over the last few days and he smiled knowingly. "I hear these kinds of stories all the time," he said. "Things will work out. But in the meantime, batten down the hatches."

"What do you mean?"

"Once you make up your mind, all hell will break loose trying to stop you. But hang in there and things will work out."

I thought it was a peculiar, if not ominous, remark, but Keri and I moved forward, locating an agency that specialized in Chinese adoptions. My cousin's words proved prophetic. Almost immediately after signing the agency contract everything seemed to go wrong with the process. At one point we were delayed for several months because a report came back that I was a convicted felon.

"How did you clear that up?" I asked the woman at the agency.

"The other Richard Paul Evans is still in prison," she replied.

After more than a year we still had no child. Then, unexpectedly, Keri got pregnant. Our last child had taken years of emotionally painful infertility treatments. This time we hadn't even been trying. We began to wonder if we were really supposed to adopt a child after all. Still, we persevered.

Nearly two years in, the biggest problem we faced was that time was running out. To begin the process we had to file for a special adoption application with the Chinese government—one that was about to expire. If it expired before we got our child, we would have to start the entire process all over again, something that I knew, after all we had been through, would be too much.

Before becoming a writer, I had been a political advertising consultant, and I personally knew most of Utah's congressional delegation. I contacted both of our US senators, who agreed to do their best to help. But nothing came from their efforts. As one said, "I'd rather work with the IRS than the INS."

Then Keri gave birth to our first son. Six days later, she experienced complications that nearly took her life. In fact, had I not happened to delay a business trip at the last moment, she likely would have bled to death in her sleep. I think it was then that we hit the wall. Our hope of adopting a Chinese child just wasn't meant to be.

Then, just a few weeks before our application was to expire, Keri said something profound. "We've relied on money and political clout to make this happen, not God. We believed that God wanted us to adopt this baby. I think we need to surrender it to Him. If God doesn't want us to adopt, we need to accept that too."

"You're saying we should just give up?" I asked her.

"No," she replied. "You know how much I want this baby. I'm saying we should give it up to God."

She was right. We had started the adoption process because we felt we had been divinely inspired. It was time to prove that we really had been. The next day we fasted to increase our spirituality. Then, that evening, we went to our church and prayed. As we drove home I said to Keri, "I feel at peace."

She nodded. "So do I."

Less than an hour later we received a call from the adoption agency. "We have a baby for you," the woman said. "You need to make your travel plans immediately and go get her before your certificate expires."

A week later I was on a plane to southern China. Keri was unable to go because of our infant son. Instead, I brought my mother-in-law.

One amusing experience I had was while I was having

dinner at the Guangzhou Hard Rock Cafe with a group of other Americans. I had never met any of them before, but they were also there to adopt. Halfway through dinner the topic of books came up. One of the women said, "My favorite author is Richard Paul Evans. Have you heard of him?"

I looked at her and realized she had no idea who I was.

"My wife likes him too," I said. "Usually."

My mother-in-law just smiled.

A few days later, we were waiting in a hotel room when the agency brought in the first baby. The situation was a little strange, as I didn't know if I was seeing my daughter for the first time or someone else's child. Struggling with English, the woman holding the baby said, "Baby E . . . Ewans."

I'll never forget calling Keri and telling her I was holding our little girl. Keri wept. She wept again when I got off the plane and put McKenna in her arms.

McKenna came from a tiny, impoverished farming village in the countryside south of Guangzhou. Her life would likely have been one of extreme poverty with few opportunities. Today, McKenna is an intelligent, beautiful young woman who has brought light and joy to our home. She is currently pursuing a doctorate.

Shakespeare was right. There *is* a "divinity that shapes our ends, rough-hew them how we will." Especially in a realm as important as the course of a child's life. If God can align the workings of the universe, is it so difficult to believe He can do the same with our lives?

LESSONS IN THE JUNGLE

I don't know what your destiny will be, but one thing I know: the only ones among you who will be really happy are those who will have sought and found how to serve.

—Albert Schweitzer, explorer and philanthropist

Our culture too often overlooks the fact that love is less a state of being than a decision—less a noun than a verb. As Dr. M. Scott Peck wrote, "Love is an act of will." And, as Kahlil Gibran said, "Work is love made visible."

I wanted to teach my teenage daughter this lesson, so I took her on a daddy-daughter trip to the Amazon jungle of Peru on a humanitarian mission. It turned into an extraordinary adventure. We hiked deep into the jungle with machetes. We caught caimans (similar to alligators) and saw giant sea otters. At one point we ran out of food and had to eat piranha. (It tastes like chicken.)

With a group of doctors and volunteers, we set up a

clinic in the city of Puerto Maldonado. For three days we served the Quechuan natives. Afterward I took Jenna to visit sites throughout the country: the legendary city of Machu Picchu, Pisac, Urubamba, and Ollantaytambo in the Sacred Valley, and the massive ruins of Sacsayhuamán in Cusco.

A week later, waiting for our flight in the Lima airport, I asked my daughter what she had learned from our trip.

"Let me think about it, Dad," she said.

Twelve hours later we were in Chicago's O'Hare International Airport waiting for our connection when I noticed that Jenna was crying. I asked her what was wrong.

She said, "Dad, we have so much and they have so little. It's not fair."

"No," I said, "it's not."

She was quiet for a moment, then said, "I know what I learned."

"What's that?"

"We love those whom we serve."

She got it. That's what I took her to the jungle for. Since then I've wondered if, perhaps, every time someone on this planet learns this lesson, God is somewhere saying, "You got it. Now you understand. That's what I sent you to the jungle for."

A LETTER TO MY CHILD ON GRADUATION

My Dear Child,

I am so very proud of you. Now, as you prepare to embark on a new journey—your own journey—I'd like to share some advice I wish I'd learned at your age:

Always remember that adversity is not a detour, it's the path. You will encounter obstacles. You will make mistakes. Be grateful for both. Your mistakes and failures will be your greatest teachers. And the only way to not make mistakes in this life is to do nothing, which is the biggest mistake of all.

Your challenges, if you'll let them, will become your greatest allies. Mountains can crush or raise you, depending on which side of the mountain you choose to stand. All history bears out that the great—those who have changed the world—have all suffered great challenges. And, more times than not, it's precisely those challenges that, in God's time, lead to triumph.

Abhor victimhood. Denounce entitlement. Neither are gifts, but rather cages to damn the soul. Everyone who has walked this earth is a victim of injustice. Everyone.

Most of all, do not be too quick to denounce your sufferings. The difficult road you are called to walk may, in fact, be your only path to success.

Remember, in the end, it is not the destination but the manner in which you walked that reveals who you are. Walk well. Walk with love. And as you walk remember, always, that I love you.

With all my affection,
Dad

THE QUEEN ANNE BABY GRAND

I didn't want a piano to begin with.

Despite my mother's faith in my musical promise, my piano career ended in childhood with Schumann's first book of annoying finger exercises.

So when Keri announced that she wanted a new piano for Mother's Day, I was less than excited.

"We have a piano," I said.

"It's a bad piano," she replied.

I couldn't argue. From my perspective there was no other kind. So when I found myself following her into the piano showroom the next day, it was with the intent of shocking her with the prices and walking out, consoling her with a "maybe someday."

Our visit to the piano store went as anticipated. Almost. Keri floated from instrument to instrument, her smile falling with each inspected price tag while I watched smugly, my wallet safely intact. *All according to plan*, I thought. Another fifteen minutes and we'd be driving home piano-free.

Then I saw it. The Queen Anne mahogany baby grand. It wasn't just a piano. It transcended piano. It was art. It was beauty. It was all that was right with the world—a piece of skillfully crafted woodmongery that had fallen from some loftier sphere into this humble showroom. It didn't matter what it sounded like. We could just put it in our living room and gaze at it.

The salesman knew love when he saw it. "She's a beaut, isn't she?" he said. "Only one in the state. It will probably be gone by morning."

Panic gripped my heart. *Someone take my piano?* For what it's worth, I consider myself a sophisticated consumer. I was, after all, an advertising executive by profession—an abuser of such transparent sales stratagems. But when one is in love, the logical portion of the brain is parked in idle. The salesman played me as masterfully as Beethoven himself might have played the celestial instrument I coveted. I pulled him aside.

"How much?" I asked, embarrassed to equate money with love.

"Should retail for twelve thousand," he said, carefully measuring my resistance like a fisherman testing the strength of his line, ". . . but we'll sell it for six. Better buy it now. It'll be gone by tomorrow."

"It's for my wife. I want to surprise her with it."

"No problem," he said.

Just then, fiscal responsibility reared its accountant-spectacled head. "I better look around first," I said mechanically. "You know . . . compare prices." I spoke haltingly, as if afraid of insulting the man.

A confident smile crossed his face. "Tell you what I'll do," he said. "I'll write up an invoice with your name on it and hold the Queen Anne until noon tomorrow. No later."

I looked across the showroom where Keri stared longingly at the beautiful instruments. The mother of our precious children. The love of my life. Our entire bank account was a small sacrifice for such a woman. This would be a Mother's Day she would never forget.

"All right," I said. "I'll see you tomorrow."

As we left the showroom, Keri put her arm in mine. "Well, maybe someday," she said sadly.

I was glassy-eyed.

By nine the next morning, I was on the phone calling all the local piano stores to investigate my desired purchase. I found the experience somewhat akin to asking a professional wrestler what he thought of his next opponent. Somehow every piano dealer offered the only credible line of pianos in the world. The one exception was Steinway; no one disputed its quality. But you cannot live inside a Steinway, and it was that or our house, so after hearing the prices, I let the salesclerk know I was not in their price stratosphere.

"But nothing plays like a Steinway," the salesclerk said.

"Including my wife," I replied as I hung up. The truth was, I was clearly out of my element. But I knew someone who spoke the language: my business partner, Evan. He would know. He was the owner of a grand piano. He could play my Queen Anne and discern its value.

With but one hour before my deadline, I dragged him from the office to see my love. He knew the piano instantly from its curves. With unfeigned reverence he sat down at the instrument, stretched his fingers, and began to play. How sweet it sounded. He was impressed. I was smitten. I wrote out a deposit. This would be a Mother's Day neither Keri nor I would ever forget.

"This is a surprise," I reminded the salesman. "Under no circumstances are there to be any calls to my house. If there are any problems, you can call me at my office."

"Understood," the man said, folding the check into his shirt pocket. "By the way," he continued, "we turn all our financing over to the local bank, so you'll be making payments to them."

"That won't be necessary," I said. "I plan to pay the piano off the day after you deliver it. I would pay it off now, except my wife would notice the change in our bank account and that would ruin the surprise."

"I still have to send the invoice to them. It's in our contract. So you'll pay them off."

Whatever, I thought.

The next morning, I told Keri I had returned to the showroom. "Our piano was sold," I said.

She was crestfallen. "Sold? In one day?"

"He said it would be gone by tomorrow."

"That's just typical sales tactics. You'd have to be dumb to fall for that."

"So you'd think," I said.

"That's too bad. I really loved that piano."

I feigned disappointment. "So did I."

In my heart I rejoiced at her disappointment. All was according to plan. At least mine. Hers was a completely different matter.

She could not have conspired to make the next two weeks more miserable for me.

The following day, Keri returned to the showroom with her sister, Shelley, to show her the one that got away.

"There it is," she said. "Rick said it was sold. They must not have delivered it yet. I wonder who bought it." She lifted the red SOLD tag and squealed. "It's sold to the EVANSES!" She turned to Shelley. "Do you really think Rick bought it?"

Fortunately, I had let Shelley in on the surprise. "No," she said. "Rick is way too cheap."

This was only the beginning of how things truly became shameless.

That afternoon, Keri called me at work. "I went out to the piano place today," she said. "There was a sold tag on our piano."

"Yes," I replied coolly. "I told you it was sold."

"The tag said 'Evans' on it."

"Oh, really?" My heart beat wildly.

"I thought maybe you had bought it. You know, to surprise me."

I detected doubt in her voice. I could still pull this off. "Wow. Sold to an Evans? What are the odds?"

"Shelley said you would never buy it because you're too cheap. But then, maybe she's in on it."

"In on what?"

"The plan."

"What plan?"

"The plan to surprise me with the piano for Mother's Day."

I breathed in deeply. "Honey, I told you that the piano was sold when I went out there. I mean, I got you something nice for Mother's Day, but it wasn't five thousand dollars!"

"Six thousand dollars," she corrected. The erroneous dollar amount was a clever insert on my part, and she fell for it. I could hear a slight tone of disappointment in her voice.

"Honey, I really don't want to ruin your Mother's Day by getting your hopes up. If you don't believe me, call the showroom and ask them who bought the piano."

My confidence dissuaded her. "Oh," she said, clearly disappointed. "Sorry to bother you at work."

"No, I'm sorry, honey. I wish I really had bought it for you."

"See you tonight."

The minute Keri hung up, I called the piano store. I scolded the salesclerk who answered the phone. "My wife was in your showroom today and saw her name on the piano I'm trying to surprise her with. I can't believe you guys put our name on it."

"We always put names on sold pianos," he said.

"It's supposed to be a surprise. I think I've convinced her that someone else named Evans bought it, but she may still call to find out. I want you to instruct all your salespeople to tell her that someone in Idaho bought it. Put a note by the phone if you have to."

"What if she doesn't call?"

"She'll call."

"What's the name?"

"My wife's name?"

"No, the person in Idaho."

"I don't care. Make one up."

"How about Lavita?"

"Lavita?"

"That's my grandmother's name," he said proudly. "She lives in Idaho."

"Whatever," I said.

My wife's persistence is near-legendary, but even I was surprised by the conversation the next morning at breakfast.

"Lavita."

I looked up from my cereal. "Lavita?"

"Lavita."

"What are you talking about?" I asked innocently.

"I called the showroom. They said they sold the piano to a Lavita Evans in Idaho." Uncomfortable pause. "Doesn't it seem peculiar that they told me the woman's name?"

"I suppose. You called the showroom?"

"You told them to say that, didn't you?"

I rolled my eyes. "Yeah, right. I called the piano store and told them to tell everyone there that my wife may call, so be sure to tell her that some woman named Lavita Evans in Idaho bought the piano."

She considered my words. "I guess you'd have to be pretty crazy to do something like that."

"Totally," I said.

Keri was quiet, but I knew she wasn't finished. She was just thinking over her next steps. It was time to act.

"Honey, I don't know how else to say this. I really wish I had bought the piano for you. I would buy it now if I could."

Keri looked at me with pity. "Well, I'm glad you didn't buy it," she finally said.

"Why is that?"

"Because it had a big scratch on it."

My chest constricted. "A scratch?"

"A deep one. All the way across the back." I felt sick to my stomach, then looked into Keri's eyes and saw them searching for my reaction. *What a devious woman*, I thought.

"Good thing we didn't buy it, then," I said calmly.

She looked at me for a moment, then walked away.

The next day, Keri called me at work.

"Honey, you'll never guess what."

You have no idea how right you are, I thought. "What?"

"A private school in Preston is closing, and guess what they're selling?"

"A piano," I ventured.

"A grand piano! And it's in mint condition! I put fifty dollars down to hold it."

"Honey, shouldn't we have talked about this first?"

"You said you would have bought the other piano if you

could have. I'm glad you didn't. I like this one just as much, and it's more than a thousand less."

My stomach churned. I was grasping here, but I was desperate. "That would be great, but a grand piano won't fit in our living room. It would stick out over the fireplace. Remember that guy said a grand piano is twenty-six inches wider than a baby grand?"

"He never said that."

"Sure he did."

The phone went quiet. "I hope they'll give me my deposit back," she finally said.

I hung up the phone and slumped over my desk. Just then my secretary, Heather, entered my office.

"More piano woes?" she asked.

"Mother's Day will never come," I said.

"Isn't it your anniversary next Friday?"

"Yes."

"If I were you, I'd have them deliver the piano on your anniversary as an early Mother's Day gift. For now, you can tell Keri you'll go look with her for a piano next Saturday."

"Great idea," I said.

It wasn't. The plan backfired miserably. The idea of unrestrained piano shopping boiled the coupon-clipping, sale-hunting consumer blood that coursed through Keri's veins. She intended to be a piano expert by Saturday. With notebook and calculator in hand, she ran to nearly every piano store in Salt Lake Valley. Ninety-six hours before V-day, Keri called my office. I was learning to dread her calls.

"I'm really glad you didn't buy that Queen Anne piano," she

said for the third time in two weeks. "I don't want it anymore. It's not a good kind."

My heart, now well-versed in the procedure, began palpitating. "Really?"

"Yeah. The manufacturer is being sued for saying their soundboard is made of hardwood when it's really not. They have a piece of particleboard sandwiched between two layers of hardwood, and the ultra-resins they use can eventually separate. Good thing I found this out before we made a big mistake."

"Soundboard," I repeated.

"Besides, I like the look of this other piano I found even better."

It's not worth it, I lamented. *Nothing is worth this.* I was about to break, to tell all, when, inexplicably, a fire of determination ignited in my chest. No, I had come too far to be denied. The wrong piano? Who cares about the piano. It was the Mother's Day surprise that mattered. She would be surprised whether she liked the piano or not. No one, not even my wife, would take this surprise from me . . . er . . . her.

"Honey, how about we go see the piano this Saturday?"

"Good idea," she said agreeably. "You will be glad you did." She hung up.

For better or worse, I had succeeded. Friday was the day of the piano delivery and the surprise of my wife's life. The mother of all Mother's Days. I had looked into the gaping jaws of defeat and spit.

Just fourteen and a half hours from my moment of triumph, the phone rang. It was Keri. "I've done something bad," she said.

"What?"

"I opened something I shouldn't have."

"Opened what?" I asked.

"A letter from a bank."

I immediately knew. The bankers. It's always the bankers. I didn't speak. I barely breathed.

"We'll laugh about it someday," she said hopefully.

"Someday?" I said hysterically. "Ha! I'm laughing now." It was the demented laugh of a man who had lied and schemed, been insulted and demeaned, only to be denied in the end. Denied his dream of the ultimate surprise—a Mother's Day of unequaled magnitude.

Then I remembered the piano. There was still the beautiful, hand-carved Queen Anne baby grand.

A calm enveloped me. Yes, the piano, the mahogany piece of heaven that would fill our home with beautiful tones of rich, familial spirituality: now more than just an instrument of beauty, it came with a story that would live in our family's history, reminding Keri and me both, each time it played, of my love for her.

No, I hadn't been denied. At least not about what really mattered. For even Keri was surprised at the lengths I was willing to go to give her a Mother's Day she would never forget—to honor her for all the beauty and joy and madness she brings to my life. And that is something truly worth celebrating.

GRANDPARENT GOGGLES

I 'm the worst kind of grandparent: the pathetic kind who will show pictures of his grandchildren to complete strangers, including people on layover in the Atlanta airport who don't speak English and look terrified as they nod approvingly. I'm especially annoying because I *know* I'm annoying and still persist. You see, my grandchildren are among the most beautiful creations to ever grace this planet, ranking with Hawaiian sunsets, Tuscan mornings, and fireworks displays.

Of course, I do allow for the slightest of possibilities that I might be a tiny bit biased, as I have known grandparents to sometimes have impaired vision when it comes to their grandchildren—grandparent goggles, if you will. (These are the same goggles that can mystically transform a scribbled crayon drawing into a Monet.)

Once, at one of my book signings, a woman dropped a photograph of a child on the table in front of me. At the risk of sounding horrible or blunt or maybe just horribly blunt, it was the homeliest child I'd ever seen. In fact, I initially thought the picture was a joke, like when people post pictures of hairless cats on the internet. But when I looked up at the woman she was beaming with pride. "Isn't he beautiful," she said. "He's my grandson."

I looked back down at the picture, then replied, "You must be so proud."

Her smile widened. "You know I am!"

And she was. And I smiled for her extraordinary vision and the power of her goggles.

I witnessed a goggle experience while picking up our adopted daughter, McKenna, in China. Another American couple was proudly showing off their new baby who, frankly, looked like an Asian version of Benjamin Button—not the hunky Brad Pitt but the creepy-old-man version.

"Can you believe how beautiful she is?" the swooning mother asked. I couldn't help but smile for her joy and good taste.

As I was holding my own daughter for the first time, the Chinese guide assisting us suddenly asked, "Do you want her?"

I looked at him quizzically. "What do you mean, do I want her?"

"Is she pretty enough?"

I was offended by the question. "Of course I want her. Why wouldn't I want her?"

"You do not know," he said in strained English. "Your baby is pretty. Maybe if she not so pretty you do not want her. Americans sometime do not want ugly babies."

Sadly, there is truth in what he said. A few decades ago, China suspended foreign adoptions for a while when an American couple refused to take their assigned baby from an orphanage because she wasn't "pretty" enough.

A few months after we brought our daughter home from China, someone who was considering a Chinese adoption called Keri to ask about the process. After talking for several minutes, the woman asked what was really on her mind.

"Is she pretty?"

"Is who pretty?" my wife asked.

"Your daughter. Is she really pretty? Is she like a china doll?"

Keri was taken aback by the question. "Yes. She's pretty."

"Do you get to look at pictures and pick your child?"

"No."

"Then how do you know if she's going to be pretty or not?"

"They're babies," Keri said. "They're all pretty."

"Oh," the woman replied, sounding disappointed. "You know what I mean . . ."

After a moment, Keri said, "You know, adopting probably isn't for you."

I was proud of my wife. Just as I'm proud of mothers and fathers and grandparents everywhere who see more through their hearts than their eyes. As Antoine de Saint-Exupéry beautifully said, "It is only with the heart that one can see rightly; what is essential is invisible to the eye."

This world doesn't need more plastic surgeons and beauty ointments. It just needs more grandparent goggles.

P.S. Want to see a picture of my grandchildren?

HOW I SAVED MY MARRIAGE

A few years ago my oldest daughter, Jenna, told me, "My greatest fear as a child was that you and Mom would get divorced. Then, about the time I was twelve, I decided that you fought so much that maybe it would be better if you did." Then she added with a smile, "I'm glad you guys figured things out."

For many years, my wife, Keri, and I struggled. Looking back, I'm not exactly sure what initially drew us together, but our personalities didn't quite match up. And the longer we were married the more extreme the differences seemed.

Encountering "fame and fortune" only exacerbated our problems. The tension between us got so bad that going out on book tours became a relief to me, though it seemed I always paid for it on reentry. Our fighting became so constant that it was difficult to even imagine a peaceful relationship. We became perpetually defensive, building emotional fortresses around our hearts. We were on the brink of divorce and discussed it more than once.

I was on tour in Atlanta when things came to a head. We had just had another big fight on the phone and Keri had hung up on me. I was alone and lonely, frustrated and angry. I had reached my limit. That's when I turned to God. Or turned on God. I don't know if you could call it prayer—maybe shouting at God isn't prayer, maybe it is—but whatever I was engaged in, I'll never forget it. I was standing in the shower in my hotel room at the Ritz-Carlton Buckhead, yelling at God that my marriage was awful and I just couldn't do it anymore.

As much as I hated the idea of divorce, the pain of being together was just too much. I was also confused. I couldn't figure out why marriage to Keri was so hard. Deep down I knew that Keri was a good person. And I was a good person. So why couldn't we get along? Why had I married someone so different from me? Why wouldn't she change?

Finally, hoarse and broken, I sat down in the shower and began to cry. In the depths of my despair, powerful inspiration came to me. *You can't change her. You can only change yourself.* At that moment I began to pray. *If I can't change* her, *God, then change* me.

I prayed late into the night. I prayed the next day on the flight home. I prayed as I walked in the door to a cold wife who, after being apart from me for two weeks, barely even acknowledged my return.

That night, as we lay in our bed, inches from each other yet still miles apart, the inspiration came. I knew what I had to do.

The next morning, I rolled over and asked, "How can I make your day better?"

Keri looked at me angrily. "What?"

"How can I make your day better?"

"You can't," she said. "Why are you asking that?"

"I mean it," I said. "I want to know what I can do to make your day better."

She looked at me cynically. "You want to do something? Go clean the kitchen."

She likely expected me to get mad. Instead I just nodded. "Okay."

I got up and cleaned the kitchen.

The next day I asked the same thing. "What can I do to make your day better?"

Her eyes narrowed. "Clean the garage."

I took a deep breath. I already had a busy day, and I knew she had said that out of spite. I was tempted to blow up at her. Instead I said, "Okay."

I got up and for the next two hours cleaned the garage. Keri wasn't sure what to think.

The next morning came. "What can I do to make your day better?"

"Nothing!" she said. "You can't do anything. Stop asking me that."

"I'm sorry," I said. "But I can't. I made a commitment to myself. What can I do to make your day better?"

"Why are you doing this?"

"Because I care about you," I said. "And our marriage."

The next morning I asked again. And the next. And the

next. Then, during the second week, a miracle occurred. As I asked the question, Keri's eyes welled up with tears. Then she broke down crying. When she could speak she said, "Please stop asking me that. You're not the problem. I am. I'm hard to live with. I don't know why you stay with me."

I gently lifted her chin until she was looking in my eyes. "It's because I love you," I said. "What can I do to make your day better?"

"I should be asking you that."

"You should," I said. "But not now. Right now I need to be the change. You need to know how much you mean to me."

She put her head against my chest. "I'm sorry I've been so mean."

"I love you," I said.

"I love you too," she replied.

"What can I do to make your day better?" I asked.

She looked at me sweetly. "Can we just spend some time together?"

I smiled. "I'd like that."

I continued asking for more than a month. And things did change. The fighting stopped. Then Keri began asking, "What do you need from me? How can I be a better wife?"

The walls between us fell. We began having meaningful discussions on what we wanted from life and how we could make each other happier. No, we didn't solve all our problems. I can't even say that we never fought again. But the nature of our fights changed. Not only were they becoming more and more rare, they lacked the energy they'd once had. We'd deprived them of oxygen. We just didn't have it in us to hurt each other anymore.

Keri and I have now been married for almost forty years. I not only love my wife, I like her. I like being with her. I need her. Many of our differences have become strengths and the others don't really matter. We've learned how to take care of each other and, more importantly, we've gained the desire to do so.

Marriage is hard. But so is parenting and keeping fit and writing books and everything else important and worthwhile in my life. To have a partner in life is a remarkable gift. I've also learned that the institution of marriage can help heal us of our most unlovable parts. And we *all* have unlovable parts.

Over time I've learned that our experience was an illustration of a much larger lesson about marriage. The question everyone in a committed relationship should ask their significant other is, "What can I do to make your life better?" That is love. Romance novels (and I've written a few) are all about desire and happily-ever-after, but happily-ever-after doesn't come from desire—at least not the kind portrayed in most pulp romances. Real love is not to desire a person but to desire their happiness—sometimes, even, at the expense of our own.

Real love is not to make another person a carbon copy of oneself. It is to expand our own capabilities of tolerance and caring, to actively seek another's well-being. All else is simply a charade of self-interest.

I'm not saying that what happened to Keri and me will work for everyone. I'm not even claiming that all marriages should be saved. But for me, I am incredibly grateful for the inspiration that came to me that day so long ago. I'm grateful that my family is still intact and that I still have my wife, my best friend, in bed next to me when I wake in the morning. And I'm grateful that even now, decades later, every now and then, one of us will still roll over and ask, "What can I do to make your day better?"

Being on either side of that question is something worth waking up for.

ACKNOWLEDGMENTS

I t would be impossible to thank all those who impacted these essays. Still, I wish to thank Simon & Schuster president and CEO Jonathan Karp for his continued interest in this collection. Also, my Gallery Books friends, Jennifer Bergstrom, Aimee Bell, Jennifer Long, and Sally Marvin. My publicist, Jessica Roth, and my marketer, Mackenzie Hickey. Also my much-adored editor, Abby Zidle, and her tireless assistant editor, Frances Yackel. Yet another thank-you to my agent, Laurie Liss, for being as excited about this book as I was. And, always, my assistant of fifteen years, Diane Glad. What a blessing it was that you came to me all those years ago.

On the home front, my wife, Keri, for living through most of these essays with me.